EZEKIEL:
The Man and The Message

By: Dr. Jimmy DeYoung

All Scripture references are taken from the *King James Version of the Holy Bible*.

Cover design by: Chad W. Smith

EZEKIEL: The Man and The Message

Copyright © 2012 by Shofar Communications, Inc. and Jimmy DeYoung.

ISBN – 978-0-9708246-3-9

PO Box 2510 Chattanooga, TN 37409

(423) 825-6247

www.prophecytoday.com

Printed in the **United States of America**.

Acknowledgments

As always, I have had much help in developing this book from the original idea through final draft. I would like to thank the usual cast of characters. Joy Martin for patiently transcribing my sermon series. Chad Smith for developing the cover art and graphics. My wife Judy for reading and re-reading the manuscript and offering valuable insight and advice. My sister-in-law Bonnie Varble for her tremendous amount of work in the editing process. Finally, my son Rick for managing the entire project.

Without this team of people, the process of putting a book together would be much more difficult for me and I would again like to express my sincerest appreciation for all their help.

Table of Contents

Introduction

I have what I consider a dear friend who has written an excellent book. I would like to study that book with you now. My good friend's name is Ezekiel. I have grown to love him like a dear brother. Ezekiel graduated from "Priest's School" after twenty-eight years to become part of the priesthood. He spent twenty-eight years studying the book of Leviticus and became very knowledgeable. At that point, God decided that He wanted him to be a prophet as well. Ezekiel had the dual responsibilities of being a priest and a prophet.

I am going to enjoy introducing Ezekiel to you. I hope that you will become as much of a friend to him as I am, or he a friend to you as he is to me. He is a true man of God. The Lord called him the "Son of man" over ninety times in the book of Ezekiel. The term "Son of man" is a very special and unique designation given by God. There is only one other person in all of history ever referred to as the "Son of man," and that is Jesus Christ Himself. In fact, Jesus Christ, in a pre-incarnate appearance, stood face to face with Ezekiel, and that is why Ezekiel had such a unique ministry and did some of the things that he did. Ezekiel was also (as far as I can discern through my study of the Word of God) the first "street preacher" in history.

Maybe some of you have read a portion of Ezekiel's book or glanced through it. I know there are programs to read through the Bible in a year, which is a remarkable feat. However, many of you do that through speed reading, and you hardly understand much of what you read. Let's be clear—that is not Bible study. Don't substitute reading through the Bible in a year with true Bible study. You need to spend time studying the Word of God. Now, even if you have, I'll bet you didn't read chapters 40 through 46 with much intensity. I say that, because those chapters are very, very detailed. But, contained in those chapters are two hundred and two verses with the most important information that God has given us about the return of the Lord Jesus Christ, and an indicator of how close that return may be.

A Foundation for Studying Bible Prophecy

A Brief Look at Bible Prophecy

Before we begin our in-depth study of Ezekiel, I would first like to give you an introduction to Bible prophecy. I want to lay a foundation for you that will be applicable in all prophetic study. Let me tell you why it is so important. Prophecy is thirty-three percent of the entire Holy Bible. Take your Bible and locate the book of Daniel. It is right after Ezekiel. Next, find the book of Revelation and go to the last chapter. Grab that portion of your Bible (Daniel 1 through Revelation 22) and put it between your thumb and your index finger. This portion of your Bible is roughly four hundred of the eleven hundred and eighty-nine chapters in the entire Word of God. Basically, you are holding thirty-three percent of the entire Word of God. This portion of pages represents how much of your Bible is prophetic in nature. One out of every three pages in the Bible consists of prophetic content. Without a doubt, a foundation in prophecy is essential for understanding all the lessons from the Bible.

In order to help you understand Bible prophecy, I am going to share with you what I like to call the Trio of Triplets. At the conclusion of this introductory study, I will tell you what we are going to be touching on as we study Bible prophecy in general, and the book of Ezekiel in particular.

THE TRIO OF TRIPLETS

THREE MAIN EVENTS OF BIBLE PROPHECY
THE RAPTURE OF THE CHURCH
THE REVELATION OF JESUS CHRIST
THE GREAT WHITE THRONE JUDGMENT

THREE STRANDS OF THE HUMAN FAMILY
GENTILES........ Genesis 1-11
JEWS .... Genesis 12 – Acts 1
CHRISTIANS .... Acts 2

THREE MAIN BOOKS OF BIBLE PROPHECY
DANIEL .... A Timeline for Gentiles
EZEKIEL .... A Timeline for Jews
REVELATION ... A Timeline for Christians

The Trio of Triplets is three sets of three's. Understanding this concept will assist you in your study of prophecy. It will not give you all the prophetic answers and knowledge, but it will enhance your understanding.

Three Main Events

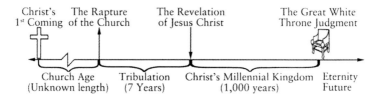

The above timeline displays the next main events on God's calendar of events. This is the first trio—the first set of three's—that I want to talk about and it's the basis, or foundation, for understanding Bible prophecy. The arrow on the left of the timeline is pointing to a period of time about six thousand years ago. That is where our timeline began.

COLOSSIANS 1:16

> For by him were all things created, that are in heaven, and that are in earth, visible and invisible, whether [they be] thrones, or dominions, or principalities, or powers: all things were created by him, and for him:

Six thousand years ago, Jesus Christ the Creator spoke the worlds into existence in six 24-hour days. History continued for four thousand years, at which point Jesus Christ was born on this earth, lived, died, was buried, resurrected, and then returned to Heaven. Another two thousand years passed, and we come to today, where we now quickly approach what will be the next main event on God's calendar—**the Rapture of the Church**.

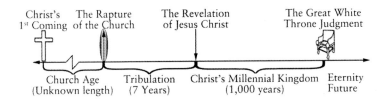

Christ's The Rapture   The Revelation   The Great White
1st Coming of the Church   of Jesus Christ   Throne Judgment

Church Age   Tribulation   Christ's Millennial Kingdom   Eternity
(Unknown length)   (7 Years)   (1,000 years)   Future

Jesus Christ will shout, the archangel will shout, the trumpet of God will sound, and we will be called up to be with Him in the air at the rapture of the church. Now, the word "rapture" is not actually used in the Bible. But that is nothing to worry about. The word "Trinity" is not used in the Bible either, nor will you find the word "Bible" used in the Bible. So, I'm not worried about the word "rapture" not being there. I am not worried, because the event is described in First Thessalonians.

I THESSALONIANS 4:13-18

But I would not have you to be ignorant, brethren, concerning them which are asleep, that ye sorrow not, even as others which have no hope.

For if we believe that Jesus died and rose again, even so them also which sleep in Jesus will God bring with him.

For this we say unto you by the word of the Lord, that we which are alive [and] remain unto the coming of the Lord shall not prevent them which are asleep.

For the Lord himself shall descend from heaven with a shout, with the voice of the archangel, and with the trump of God: and the dead in Christ shall rise first:

Then we which are alive [and] remain shall be caught up together with them in the clouds, to meet the Lord in the air: and so shall we ever be with the Lord.

Wherefore comfort one another with these words.

The apostle Paul said that we shall be caught up to be with Him in the air. Jesus Christ had mentioned the rapture to his disciples on the night before he was crucified. They were so anxious that night that it went right over their heads and they did not understand it at all.

JOHN 14:1-3

Let not your heart be troubled: ye believe in God, believe also in me.

In my Father's house are many mansions: if [it were] not [so], I would have told you. I go to prepare a place for you.

And if I go and prepare a place for you, I will come again, and receive you unto myself; that where I am, [there] ye may be also.

These verses are not talking about the second coming of Jesus Christ. The Revelation (or second coming) is an entirely different event. To be "received where He is" is talking about the rapture of the church. The rapture is the next main event in God's calendar of activities.

After the rapture, there is going to be a seven-year period of time called the time of Tribulation. This is talked about in Revelation 4:2 - 19:10. Throughout those sixteen chapters of Revelation is detailed information about this terrible time of Tribulation. The word "church" is used in the book of Revelation twenty-five times. It is used nineteen times before Revelation 4:1 (when the rapture takes place) and it is used six times after Revelation 19:22 (when the revelation, or second coming, of Christ takes place). The word "church" is not used at all in those sixteen chapters (Revelation 4:2 - 19:10) describing the terrible time of judgment during the Tribulation period. That indicates to me that either God forgot to put us in the Tribulation or we are not supposed to be there. I would have to say it's the latter: we are not supposed to be there.

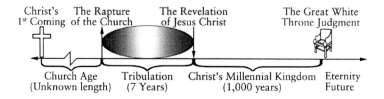

After the Tribulation, Jesus Christ gets on a white horse, as do we, and comes back. That event is called— *the Revelation of Jesus Christ (or more commonly, the second coming).*

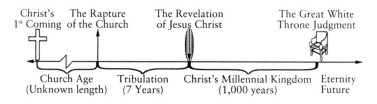

Following the Revelation, there will be a thousand-year period of time (the Millennium), which will be followed by the last of the three main events—*the Great White Throne Judgment.* This event, then, is followed by eternity future, which includes a new heaven, a new earth, and a new Jerusalem.

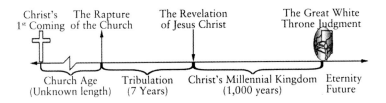

Now we have a roadmap through eschatology, a pathway through the end times where we clearly see that the rapture of the church is the next event to take place. We are currently living at a time in history just prior to the rapture. Remember to keep this roadmap in mind as we study the book of Ezekiel.

That's the first set of three's. I promise that if you get this trio of triplets, you will be able to understand how to approach the study of Bible prophecy.

Three Strands of the Human Family

To get us started on the second set of three's, come with me to the tenth chapter in First Corinthians. Now I know that this is not a prophetic passage of Scripture. It is talking about Paul relating to a very carnal church.

I CORINTHIANS 10:23
All things are lawful for me, but all things are not expedient: ....

I understand what Paul is teaching here, but I am going to take it out of context just for a moment. It will lay a foundation stone on which we can build our study of prophecy.

Paul, in his message to the people of Corinth, said that *"All things are lawful for me, but all things are not expedient."* If you continue reading, you'll find out why he makes that statement.

I CORINTHIANS 10:32

> *Give none offence, neither to the Jews, nor to the Gentiles, nor to the church of God:*

What Paul is saying, is that there are three members of the human family. There are Gentiles, there are Jews, and there is the church of God. (For simplicity, I will refer to *"the church of God"* as "Christians"—meaning true, Bible-believing, born-again Christians; blood-bought believers, who are going to be with Christ forever and ever.)

So, we find that there are three strands of the human family—Gentiles, Jews, and Christians.

THREE STRANDS
OF THE HUMAN FAMILY

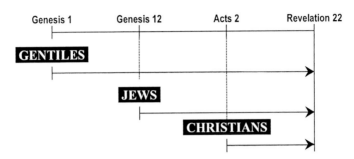

In the first two thousand years of human history, there were only Gentiles on the earth. When God created Adam and Eve, they were Gentiles. The word for "Gentiles" in Hebrew is "goy" or "goyim," and it's first used in the tenth chapter of Genesis.

GENESIS 10:5

By these were the isles of the Gentiles divided in their lands; every one after his tongue, after their families, in their nations.

Genesis 10:5 is discussing the genealogies of Shem, Ham, and Japheth (the sons of Noah) after the flood. For the first two thousand years, from Genesis 1 to Genesis 11, there were only Gentiles upon the face of the earth. You might ask, "Were there believers in that time?" The answer is, "Yes." Seth, the son of Adam was a believer.

GENESIS 4:25-26

And Adam knew his wife again; and she bare a son, and called his name Seth: For God, [said she,] hath appointed me another seed instead of Abel, whom Cain slew.

And to Seth, to him also there was born a son; and he called his name Enos: then began men to call upon the name of the LORD.

Notice in verse 26 that it says, "*then began men to call upon the name of the LORD.*" You cannot call upon the Lord unless the message has been presented, and how can the message be presented unless someone delivers it from God. Seth was a great preacher and men started to call upon the name of the Lord due to his preaching. However, Seth was not a Christian. He was a Gentile believer.

Enoch was also an outstanding preacher.

GENESIS 5:24

And Enoch walked with God: and he [was] not; for God took him.

JUDE 14-15

And Enoch also, the seventh from Adam, prophesied of these, saying, Behold, the Lord cometh with ten thousands of his saints,

To execute judgment upon all, and to convince all that are ungodly among them of all their ungodly deeds which they have ungodly committed, and of all their hard [speeches] which ungodly sinners have spoken against him.

Enoch preached about the coming of the Messiah. But he was not a Christian. He was a believing Gentile.

Noah preached one hundred and twenty years before the Great Flood. He was a great preacher. He was a great believer. God called him to a position to be used in a mighty way. But he was not a Christian. He was a Gentile believer. This is an important point for us to understand. There are no Christians in the first twelve chapters of the book of Genesis. All you have are Gentiles—some believing and some lost.

In the twelfth chapter of the book of Genesis, we see the second two-thousand-year period of history begin to unfold. God reaches into Ur of the Chaldees and finds a man named Abram. God brings him up over the Fertile Crescent (modern-day Syria), down the Rift Valley (which extends from Syria in the north to Kenya in the south), through the Jordan Valley, and into the land of Canaan (modern-day Israel). God brings Abram, whose name was ultimately changed to Abraham, into the land and He is going to establish another strand of the human family. In fact, Abraham was the first to be referred to as a Hebrew.

GENESIS 14:13

And there came one that had escaped, and told Abram the Hebrew; for he dwelt in the plain of Mamre the Amorite, brother of Eshcol, and brother of Aner: and these [were] confederate with Abram.

So Abraham was the first to be referred to as Hebrew. Abraham's grandson, Jacob, was the first to be referred to as Israel (Genesis 32:28). Abraham's great-grandson, Judah, was the first one to be called a Jew (II Kings 16:6). Here we see that God is establishing the second strand of the human family—the Jews. For the first two thousand years there were Gentiles. Then, starting in Genesis 12 and extending through Acts 1, in addition to the Gentiles, a second strand has come into existence—the Jews.

I love to use opportunity evangelism. What I do is I just simply wait for an opportunity to come along in a conversation and then I go right to Jesus. (Now, if the opportunity does not come, I make the opportunity!) A few years ago I was sitting on a boat on the Sea of Galilee. This particular boat was called "the Jesus boat." It was a replica of the boat that Jesus would have sailed in while fishing on the Sea of Galilee. During this time I met a lovely Jewish lady. She was robust, vibrant, and joyful. She had heard me talking to our tour group on the boat and knew I was talking about Jesus. All of a sudden, she turned to me and said,

"I don't know what's wrong with you Christians!"

"What do you mean, ma'am?" I replied.

She said, "Don't you know the first Christian was a Jew?"

"That's right, that's good. I like that. Oh, that's great, I'm going to use that in my teaching," I said.

She was so pleased. She just sat back to bask in her pride. I was letting her enjoy it a little bit. When everything quieted down, I looked over at her and said,

"I don't know what's wrong with you Jews!"

"What do you mean, son?" she replied.

I said, "Don't you know the first Jew was a Gentile?"

"He was?" she asked. "How did that happen?"

I said, "Glad you asked me, ma'am," and I took her to the Word.

Abraham was a Gentile. God brought him into the land that He was to give to Abraham, Isaac, Jacob, and their descendants—the Jewish people. God established the Jews as a special people unto Himself. The Bible tells us in Deuteronomy that it was not because they were going to be obedient, not because they were going to be loving, and not because they were going to honor Him. In fact, they were going to be hard-headed, hard-hearted, and stiff-necked. God selected the Jews because He loved them. Deuteronomy 32:8 says that God *"set the bounds of the people according to the number of the children of Israel."* Then, He set the nations and countries of the world around these special people in the city of Jerusalem, which is the center of the earth (Ezekiel 5:5). He does all this for a special purpose that will be revealed as we continue our study of Ezekiel.

So there you have the first two strands of the human family—Gentiles and Jews. These two strands extend from Genesis 12 through Acts 1. In Matthew, Mark, Luke, John, and through the first chapter of Acts, there are no Christians. There were only believing Gentiles and believing Jews. Christians do not come on the scene until Acts 2, when the day of Pentecost occurs and we are baptized in the body of Christ and sealed. Believers were first called "Christians" in Acts 11:26.

> ACTS 11:26
>
> *And when he had found him, he brought him unto Antioch. And it came to pass, that a whole year they assembled themselves with the church, and taught much people. And the disciples were called Christians first in Antioch.*

The fact that there are no Christians until Acts 2 is key if you are going to understand Bible prophecy. In Matthew 24, Christians are not present; therefore, we can determine that this chapter is not talking about the rapture of the church. Matthew 24 details the revelation of Jesus Christ (the second coming). Placing the rapture in Matthew 24 will cause you to become disoriented in your understanding of Bible prophecy. We must understand this principle—there are Gentiles and Jews from Genesis 12, all the way through Acts 1. In Acts 2, the church was formed and gave us the third strand of the human family—Christians.

Gentiles, Jews, and Christians have been in existence for the last two thousand years.

Three Books of Bible Prophecy

As we continue to study our Trio of Triplets, we come to our third Triplet. For this last set of three's, I want us to look at the three books of the Bible that are the timelines for the three strands of the human family. These three books are Daniel, Ezekiel, and Revelation.

THREE MAIN BOOKS OF BIBLE PROPHECY

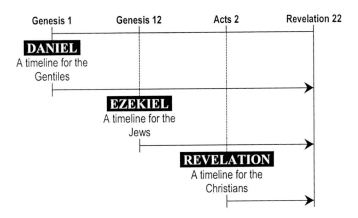

Let's look first at the book of Revelation. It begins at the resurrection of Jesus Christ.

REVELATION 1:18

[I am] he that liveth, and was dead; and, behold, I am alive for evermore,....

As you continue to study Revelation, there is a special emphasis placed on Christians, as their history progresses into eternity future. Revelation is a timeline for Christians.

Next, we look at the book of Daniel. Daniel was taken into Babylonian captivity with his three friends: Hananiah, Mishael, and Azariah (the Hebrew names of Shadrach, Meshach, and Abednego). This event took place in 605 B.C., and that marks the beginning of the timeline for the Gentiles. The book of Daniel lays out the timeline for the Gentiles from the Babylonian captivity all the way into eternity future. The book of Daniel has twelve chapters of detailed information about the Gentile world; how it is going to unfold and, ultimately, how it will conclude. In fact, one of the reasons for the Tribulation period is to bring an end to the times of the Gentiles, the times when a Gentile has control over the Jewish people and the city of Jerusalem. This was conveyed to Daniel through Nebuchadnezzar's dream (Daniel 2) and Daniel's own dream (Daniel 7).

If the book of Revelation is the timeline for the Christians and the book of Daniel is the timeline for the Gentiles, then that leaves the book of Ezekiel as the timeline for the Jews. As we continue our study of Ezekiel, you will find this to be true.

The Importance of the Trio of Triplets

THE TRIO OF TRIPLETS

THREE MAIN EVENTS OF BIBLE PROPHECY
THE RAPTURE OF THE CHURCH
THE REVELATION OF JESUS CHRIST
THE GREAT WHITE THRONE JUDGMENT

THREE STRANDS OF THE HUMAN FAMILY
GENTILES........ Genesis 1-11
JEWS .... Genesis 12 – Acts 1
CHRISTIANS .... Acts 2

THREE MAIN BOOKS OF BIBLE PROPHECY
DANIEL .... A Timeline for Gentiles
EZEKIEL .... A Timeline for Jews
REVELATION... A Timeline for Christians

If you will incorporate the Trio of Triplets in your study of Bible prophecy, it will help you to understand what is taking place in the Scriptures. For example, if you are studying a prophecy in the book of Isaiah, you can know that the prophecy is not talking about Christians—only Gentiles and Jews. I stated earlier that Matthew 24 is a prophecy only to the Jewish people, which may lead you to ask, "Isn't the Bible applicable for everybody?" Well, the Bible is applicable for everybody. There is a spiritual application in the entire Bible, but there is a technical interpretation for every page in the Bible, as well.

Let me illustrate that point by looking at the book of Leviticus. As we learned earlier, Ezekiel would have studied Leviticus in his preparation to become a priest.

He would have learned that the first seven chapters of the book of Leviticus describe the system of sacrifices. In chapters 8 through 11 of Leviticus, he would have learned the standards for the priest. Finally, chapters 12 through 27 describe the system of worship in the Tabernacle or Temple. The book of Leviticus is not technically interpreted for us as Christians. Christians do not go to a Temple, nor have a priest who leads a service, nor go through a sacrificial system. The systems described in Leviticus are technically interpreted for the Jewish people. Why, then, should we as Christians study Leviticus? The word "holiness" is used eighty-three times in the book of Leviticus. If you want to understand the holiness of God, study the book of Leviticus. Do you see my point? You can make that same hermeneutical principle apply to Matthew 24. There is some great spiritual truth there, but it is technically interpreted for the Jewish people; and it is the revelation of Christ (the second coming), not the rapture of the church.

Ezekiel as Apocalyptic Literature

Ezekiel is one of four books in the Bible that are referred to as apocalyptic literature. The word "apocalyptic" comes from the Greek word "apocalypses," which means a prophetic disclosure or a revelation. The four apocalyptic books are: Ezekiel, Daniel, Zechariah, and Revelation. Apocalyptic literature uses symbols to communicate an absolute truth. As we continue our study of Ezekiel, we will see several illustrations of apocalyptic literature. God uses symbols to communicate an absolute truth, and when He does that, He will use the Word of God to interpret that absolute truth.

An example of apocalyptic literature can be seen in the very first chapter of Ezekiel.

EZEKIEL 1:1

> Now it came to pass in the thirtieth year, in the fourth [month], in the fifth [day] of the month, as I [was] among the captives by the river of Chebar, [that] the heavens were opened, and I saw visions of God.

God is going to communicate something to this young man who was just thirty years of age. The Word of God tells us that he is a priest (Ezekiel 1:3), and that he goes to the Chebar River. The Chebar River is a tributary of the Euphrates River, located in an area known in Biblical times as Mesopotamia. Mesopotamia means "land between the rivers," and the rivers in this instance were the Tigris and the Euphrates. When Ezekiel was held captive, he was taken to the plains of Shinar, between the Tigris and the Euphrates, in Mesopotamia. This location is just outside a city called Babylon. On modern-day borders, this location is in the heart of Iraq. The book of Ezekiel takes place in Iraq. This fact is amazing to me when I think about how relevant and up-to-date the Word of God is today. The focus of the world today is on the little state of Iraq in the Middle East and the events taking place there.

To further illustrate the importance of the setting in which the book of Ezekiel is written, let us look at the background of that area. Jesus made the following statement:

> MATTHEW 24:37
> *But as the days of Noe [were], so shall also the coming of the Son of man be.*

Jesus says "*the days of Noe*" (or "Noah"). What are "the days of Noah" and where was Noah living in his last days? "The days of Noah" are the times in which Noah lived. If we go back to the book of Genesis we see that Noah lived six hundred years before the flood. Those were "the days of Noah" before the flood. Noah lived just more than a year during the flood and then he lived for three hundred and fifty years after the flood. In Genesis 9:29, we see that "all the days of Noah" were nine hundred and fifty years. In Matthew, I believe Jesus was referring to "the days of Noah" after the flood.

Where did Noah live? He lived where his great-grandson, Nimrod, built a city in the face of God. Nimrod went to the shores of the Euphrates River in Mesopotamia, right there in the plains of Shinar, and built a great city called Babylon. That's where Ezekiel and his ten thousand Jewish worshippers are going to be taken during their captivity. This location is an unbelievable eye-opener as we study the book of

Ezekiel. Ezekiel, twenty-five hundred years ago, pre-wrote history that's happening today, from the location where our world is currently focused, at exactly where it all culminates—Babylon. Revelation 18, where God passes final judgment on the city of Babylon, is the last prophetic event that Jesus Christ deals with before he steps back on planet Earth. This is the location where we find Ezekiel as he begins to write this amazing, prophetic book.

How to Study the Bible

Bible teacher Dr. Lehman Strauss is one of my heroes. Before the Lord called him home in 1997, Dr. Strauss wrote eighteen books, pastored a church, and taught the Bible all over the world. One day, I went to him and I said, "Dr. Strauss, you are so knowledgeable of the Word of God and you are such a prolific author. When you approach writing a book or teaching a book of the Bible, how do you go about it?" Dr. Strauss said, "Jimmy, the first thing I do, I read the entire book one hundred times before I ever start to teach it or write about it." That's a great Bible study tip. Specifically, he would read the entire book at one sitting. He wouldn't read a couple of chapters of Ezekiel today, and a couple of chapters tomorrow. Instead, he would sit and read the entire book of Ezekiel at one sitting. By the time he had read Ezekiel one hundred times, he had begun memorizing it in his mind. This exercise gave him the proper perspective when studying the Bible.

Dr. Strauss continued, "The second thing I do is, I put an outline with the book, because if I cannot see the overall big picture, I'm never going to be able to get all the little details. You don't go in and start inspecting the trees in the forest until you can see the forest from afar." I believe this method of study works very effectively, so I have put together an outline of the book of Ezekiel for you.

An Outline and Preview of the Book of Ezekiel

I am going to give you a suggested outline for the book of Ezekiel, the outline that this book will follow. You do not have to use my outline. In fact, my sincere hope is that this book is just the beginning of your study of Bible prophecy and you will want to develop your own outline of Ezekiel.

Ezekiel is divided into two main sections:

A MESSAGE OF RETRIBUTION
TO ISRAEL................................ Chapters 1-24
TO ISRAEL'S NEIGHBORS ....Chapters 25-32

A MESSAGE OF RESTORATION
OF THE JEWISH PEOPLE ....Chapters 33-39
OF JEWISH PRACTICES.............Chapters 40-48

We are going to use this outline as we look at the message of retribution that God gives to the street preacher, Ezekiel. I suggest that you read Ezekiel 4, 5, and 24 to see exactly how God used this unique man. Also, I am going to give you the secret as to how Ezekiel was able to accomplish so much for the glory of God (found in the first chapter of Ezekiel). I will show you how you can make this same principle applicable for yourself.

In chapter 28, Ezekiel discusses the establishment of the kingdom of this world under a being that God created; one who was first known as Lucifer, but was then given the name of Satan. We will see why angels are important in Bible prophecy. The most-used word in the book of Revelation is "angels" (it is used eighty-seven times). We will study angels and how they came into existence. We will also look at the two different sets of angels—good angels and evil angels. Evil angels will play a large role in end-time prophecy, and their involvement begins in Ezekiel 28.

In Ezekiel 34, we see God's promises to Israel. Eighteen times God gives a promise to the Jewish people in chapter 34. We see the fulfillment of one of those promises in Ezekiel 37 (the promise made in Ezekiel 34:13 to bring them back into the land). I believe that the return of Israel to the land is the most unique sign that the return of Jesus Christ to the earth is imminent.

Ezekiel 35 talks about the Palestinian people of today. The creation of a peace treaty with the Palestinians is in the news constantly today. World leaders and the United Nations have set the formation of this peace as one of their top priorities. Chapter 35 tells us how this issue will finally be resolved.

In Ezekiel 37, we are also going to study about two Jewish states. In the end times, before Christ comes back, there are going to be two Jewish states. Events are taking place right now that are setting the stage for the formation of that second Jewish state. In Northern Israel, the Israeli Defense Force is dealing with Jewish settlers who are going to move to establish this second Jewish state. Ezekiel wrote about this event over twenty-five hundred years ago.

Ezekiel 38 talks about a group of nations that will come against Israel in the last days. When I mention the nations, you will recognize every single one of them as major players today. We are going to look at how the peace process that they are calling for is going to come to fruition.

In Ezekiel 39, we will look at what is going to happen to the religion of Islam. Islam, I believe, is a satanic religion in every aspect of its being. I know this statement is not politically correct, but I believe it to be Biblically correct. I'm going to tell you what is going to happen to the Islamic world and how soon it's going to take place. All this information is found in the book of Ezekiel.

In the last chapters of Ezekiel, we will study another very significant sign that Jesus Christ is about to return—the preparations for rebuilding the Jewish Temple.

Ezekiel: A Unique Prophet

As we learned in the preceding chapter, the next main event on God's calendar of events is the rapture of the church. There is not one prophecy that has to be fulfilled before this event can take place. I was in a prophecy conference with Dr. John Walvoord, the former president of Dallas Theological Seminary and one of the leading scholars on Bible prophecy in the twentieth century. I was talking to Dr. Walvoord and he told me that a publisher had asked him to write a book about all of the prophecies in the Word of God. I asked him, "Well, are there any prophecies that have to be fulfilled before the rapture?" He said, "Jimmy, there are absolutely no prophecies that must be fulfilled before the rapture of the church. Every prophecy in the Bible that has yet to be fulfilled happens after the rapture of the church."

What we are going to learn from the prophetic book of Ezekiel pertains to events that will happen after the rapture of the church. The body of Christ will have left this world and gone into the heavens.

A Look at Genealogies and Events

Matthew 1:1-17 is a genealogy. It is from Abraham to Jesus Christ. You can learn some great things in genealogies, if you study them. The last verse is basically a summation of the genealogy.

MATTHEW 1:17

So all the generations from Abraham to David [are] fourteen generations; and from David until the carrying away into Babylon [are] fourteen generations; and from the carrying away into Babylon unto Christ [are] fourteen generations.

This verse is unique among genealogies because it deals with person to person to historic event to person. Most genealogies that I have ever read deal with people, not historic events. But within the context of this particular genealogy, we learn that the Babylonian captivity was a very unique event.

Ezekiel was a product of the Babylonian captivity. Ezekiel was taken into captivity at about thirty years of age. He was living in Jerusalem in 597 B.C., roughly eight years after Daniel and his three Hebrew friends were taken captive. God allows the Babylonians, under Nebuchadnezzar, to take Ezekiel and about ten thousand of his Jewish countrymen to Babylon. This marks the second of three waves of captives being taken to Babylon. Ezekiel is transported to the Chebar River, to a place called Tel Aviv. (This Tel Aviv is not what we know as modern-day Tel Aviv. Modern-day Tel Aviv was named after a book by Theodor Herzl, the father of Zionism.) The Babylonians took Ezekiel to Tel Aviv, where he then ministered among the Jewish people. The first chapter in Ezekiel tells us that he was a priest.

EZEKIEL 1:3

The word of the Lord came expressly unto Ezekiel the priest, the son of Buzi, in the land of the Chaldeans by the river Chebar; and the hand of the Lord was there upon him.

So, we see that Ezekiel was a priest that God was going to make a prophet as well. There are two other men in the Bible who were both priest and prophet—Jeremiah and Zechariah. Although Ezekiel studied to be a priest, he never was able to practice the priesthood because of the Babylonian captivity. Zechariah received his training during the Babylonian captivity and then he returned to Jerusalem with the ministry of encouraging the people to rebuild the Temple.

Diasporas and Aliyahs

When we talk about the Babylonian captivity, we are talking about a period of time when the Jews were taken out of their land. There are three times in history when the Jews are taken out of their land (or left the land for another purpose). In the book of Genesis, Jacob takes his family of seventy members and they head south out of Israel into Egypt. That is the first departure or Diaspora. "Diaspora" is a Greek word which means "a scattering (of seeds)" and represents the Jewish people being dispersed from their land. This Diaspora ends when we see God allowing Joshua to bring the children of Israel back into their land.

JOSHUA 3:17

And the priests that bare the ark of the covenant of the LORD stood firm on dry ground in the midst of Jordan, and all the Israelites passed over on dry ground, until all the people were passed clean over Jordan.

When they came back into the land, as depicted in the book of Joshua, that was the first return or Aliyah. "Aliyah" is a Hebrew word that literally means "to ascend (to Jerusalem)." Making Aliyah was the responsibility of every Jewish man because of the three pilgrim feasts—Passover, Pentecost, and Tabernacles. Every year as they celebrated these feasts, Jewish men had to make Aliyah. They had to go up to Jerusalem to the Temple. There, they would worship during that period of time that they were observing the feast. The word Aliyah in modern times has come to mean the process of immigrating to Israel.

The first Diaspora is in Genesis, when Jacob took seventy members of his family out of the land. Four hundred and thirty years later, Moses led them out of Egypt and back toward the Promised Land. Because of his disobedience, Moses was not allowed to enter the land. But Joshua, his first lieutenant, did return to the land. During the Exodus, when the children of Israel escaped Egyptian bondage and were wandering in the wilderness, there were two million Jews. What started as seventy became two million. The text tells us in the book of Exodus that there were six hundred thousand men, plus the women and children. If you have six hundred thousand men, you probably have six hundred thousand women as well. Who wants to go anyplace without your woman, right? And, if you have six hundred thousand men and six hundred thousand women, you probably have one million kids. You can understand what drove Moses crazy.

The second Diaspora of the Jewish people started in 605 B.C., when Daniel and the three Hebrews leave the land. The second phase of that Diaspora occurs in 597 B.C., when Ezekiel is taken. Finally, in 586 B.C., all the Jews are taken out of the land and into Babylonian captivity—except for Jeremiah, who went to Egypt. That is the second Diaspora. Seventy years after Daniel left, they were able to come back into the land. Isaiah 45 says that Cyrus will be raised up to allow the Jews to go back to Jerusalem and to build their Temple. That is exactly what happened. The book of Ezra records the fulfillment of that prophecy, with Zerubbabel taking about fifty thousand Jewish people—49,897 to be exact (Ezra 2:64-65)—back into the land for the purpose of rebuilding the Temple. So that was the second departure and the second return; the second Diaspora and Aliyah.

The third Diaspora was in 70 A.D. As Jesus Christ predicted (Luke 19:41-44 and Matthew 24), the Temple was destroyed and the Jews were dispersed throughout the world.

MATTHEW 24:2

And Jesus said unto them, See ye not all these things? verily I say unto you, There shall not be left here one stone upon another, that shall not be thrown down.

I have spoken with Meir Ben-Dov, the chief archeologist on the Temple Mount. I asked him directly, "Is there one stone upon another stone on this Temple Mount? In all of your searching, have you found one?"

His response: "Absolutely not."

So the prophecy in Matthew 24, that there will not be a stone upon a stone from the Temple, was fulfilled in 70 A.D. That is the third Diaspora of the people being taken out of the land and God promised a third Aliyah. God says eighteen times in Ezekiel 34 that He will bring them back into the land. This prophecy was fulfilled in 1948 when God miraculously reached into the four corners of the earth, gathered his people, and brought them back into the land. Ezekiel is absolute evidence of prophecies being fulfilled. God reached into Europe, Russia, and Ethiopia to specifically fulfill Bible prophecy and bring His people back to their land. I have studied the Word from Genesis 1:1 to Revelation 22:21, and there is never another departure out of the land or return to the land. We are living in the times talked about in the book of Ezekiel. The third and final Aliyah is in the process of unfolding before our very eyes.

As we can clearly see, God has a plan for Israel. And we are witnessing end-times prophecy being fulfilled every day when we open a newspaper and read what is taking place in the Middle East and in the world. There are, however, prominent Bible teachers in the Christian community today who believe that God is finished with the nation of Israel as a whole, and the Jewish people in particular. Much of this movement is centered on the so-called "emerging church," which basically says that Christians have replaced the Jewish people because the Jews rejected Jesus Christ. This theology is called "replacement theology." This line of thinking essentially began with Martin Luther during the Reformation and has led to many horrific acts of anti-Semitism down through the centuries. If you are in a church that says that God is done with the Jews or His program for the Jewish people is completed, I would suggest that you get out of that church immediately. God has not completed His program with the Jews. God made a promise to me, as a Christian, just as He made a promise to the Jewish people, and I expect Him to fulfill them both.

The Time of the Prophet

The Babylonian captivity is when Ezekiel received this message. What is unique about that genealogy from Abraham to Jesus (Matthew 1:17) is the reference to the Babylonian captivity, because it is the period of time when the Jews came under control of the Gentile world.

LUKE 21:24
*And they shall fall by the edge of the sword,
and shall be led away captive into all nations:*

31

and Jerusalem shall be trodden down of the Gentiles, until the times of the Gentiles be fulfilled.

As prophesied by Daniel, when the Tribulation period is unfolding, with the Jews back in the land for the third time, the times of the Gentiles will come to an end.

By the way, it is good to understand when the prophets prophesied. Two prophets prophesied during that Babylonian captivity—Ezekiel is one of them, Daniel is the other. There were three prophets who prophesied after the return from the Babylonian captivity—Haggai, Zechariah, and Malachi (the last three prophets in the Old Testament). The remaining twelve prophets in the Old Testament all prophesied prior to the Babylonian captivity.

A True Prophet versus a False Prophet

As we continue our study of Ezekiel, I would like to look at Ezekiel's qualifications to be a prophet. God is going to raise up this Jewish priest as a prophet to his own people. Those people recognized the fact that he was going to be a prophet. Eventually they understood what God was saying to them as they saw all of Ezekiel's prophecies fulfilled. Complete accuracy is what determines a true prophet. Every single prophecy made by a true prophet of God will be fulfilled in absolute detail without any deviation.

DEUTERONOMY 18:20-22

But the prophet, which shall presume to speak a word in my name, which I have not commanded him to speak, or that shall speak in the name of other gods, even that prophet shall die.

And if thou say in thine heart, How shall we know the word which the LORD hath not spoken?

When a prophet speaketh in the name of the LORD, if the thing follow not, nor come to pass, that [is] the thing which the Lord hath not spoken, [but] the prophet hath spoken it presumptuously: thou shalt not be afraid of him.

The consolation prize—or "close, but no cigar" reward—does not apply to Bible prophecy. There is only one way you can truly be a spokesperson for God and that is for all of your prophecies to be fulfilled in absolute detail.

There is a so-called television evangelist who said that the United States of America was going to be attacked at a specific time, and hundreds of thousands of people were going to be killed. That man became a heretic and a liar when that prophecy was not fulfilled. I would suggest that he's had many other prophecies that were complete frauds. In fact, when he initially gave that prophecy, he said, "You know, I've given other prophecies in the past and I missed it just a little bit." Missed it just a little bit? That's like a heart surgeon saying, "Oh, I missed that just a little bit. I'm sorry." That so-called evangelist became automatically disqualified when he made that statement. He is one of many false prophets in the world today.

Why do I bring this up? Because the Bible talks about false prophets and how we had better be aware of them. Jesus Christ, two days before he was crucified, gave the Olivet Discourse on the Mount of Olives. When asked, in Matthew 24:3, what the primary sign would be for His return (not the rapture of the church; remember, Matthew 24 is part of the timeline for the Jewish people and the revelation, or second coming, of Jesus Christ), Jesus answered as follows:

MATTHEW 24:4-5, 11, and 24
And Jesus answered and said unto them, Take heed that no man deceive you.

For many shall come in my name, saying, I am Christ; and shall deceive many.

...

And many false prophets shall rise, and shall deceive many.

...

For there shall arise false Christs, and false prophets, and shall shew great signs and wonders; insomuch that, if [it were] possible, they shall deceive the very elect.

Deception is a major sign of the soon coming of Jesus Christ.

That deception, according to Matthew 24:24, will be made manifest in signs, wonders, and miracles. There is a proliferation today of signs, wonders, and miracles.

You may say, "Jimmy, don't you believe that Jesus can do a miracle?" I believe Jesus can do anything he wants to do. I don't tell Jesus what He can do. If I could tell Jesus what He can do, that would make me God and Him, my servant. That is not the case. There is one thing I know for sure: I am not God. You can write that down and take it to the bank—I am not God. So, I'm not going to tell Jesus what He can do. I can tell you what Jesus said: deceptions, signs, wonders, and miracles are all indicators of the soon return of Christ.

I do not want to be hypocritical on this issue. The first person you'd better be watching very closely is Jimmy DeYoung. You check me out to make sure that I stay in accord with the Word of God. If I don't, I give you permission to take me to the wall. All of prophecy is contained within the Bible, between the pages of Genesis 1:1 and Revelation 22:21. There is no other prophecy outside of the Bible. Be careful of people who go outside of God's Word and want to give you some so-called prophetic truth. That is the number one sign that Jesus is coming soon.

Ezekiel's Special Name and Calling

God raised a prophet—a true prophet—in Ezekiel. Notice what it says at the beginning of the following verse:

> EZEKIEL 2:3
> *And he said unto me, Son of man, ...*

The phrase "Son of man" is God's special name for Ezekiel. That phrase is used ninety-three times in the book of Ezekiel. The only other person in the Bible that phrase is used in correlation with is Jesus Christ. Even then, the term "Son of man" is only used seventy-nine times in the New Testament. This is an example of the special relationship God had with this man, Ezekiel.

EZEKIEL 2:3 (continued)

... I send thee to the children of Israel, to a rebellious nation that hath rebelled against me: they and their fathers have transgressed against me, [even] unto this very day.

In this verse, God is talking about His Chosen people—the Jews. He is going to send a Jewish man to His people.

EZEKIEL 2:4

For [they are] impudent children and stiffhearted. I do send thee unto them; and thou shalt say unto them, Thus saith the Lord GOD.

The term *"thus saith the Lord GOD"* is used three hundred and seventeen times in the book of Ezekiel. It is intended to reference the Word of God.

EZEKIEL 2:5-6

And they, whether they will hear, or whether they will forbear, (for they [are] a rebellious house,) yet shall know that there hath been a prophet among them.

*And thou, son of man, be not afraid of them,
neither be afraid of their words, though briers
and thorns [be] with thee, and thou dost dwell
among scorpions: be not afraid of their words,
nor be dismayed at their looks, though they [be]
a rebellious house.*

I love what God says here, "Whether they listen or
not, still go tell them." God tells Ezekiel that they are
going to mock him and make fun of him, but that he still
must go. This is a great example for us to follow as we
obey God's commandment to reach the world with the
Gospel.

The second half of verse 6 can almost be
characterized as anti-Semitic. This is God talking about
the people He chose—hard-headed, stiff-necked,
impudent, like *"scorpions: be not afraid of their words,
nor be dismayed at their looks, though they [be] a
rebellious house."* Again, we get nervous when we talk to
somebody about Jesus Christ because they make a
funny look at us. Sometimes those we witness to attack
us verbally. God says, "Don't worry about that!"

I am convinced that the reason God called me and
my wife to go Israel to do difficult missionary work is
because I'm about as hard headed as any person that I
have ever come into contact with there. Witnessing
about Jesus Christ in a Jewish state is difficult, but we
take comfort in what God said in Ezekiel 3.

EZEKIEL 3:8-9

Behold, I have made thy face strong against their faces, and thy forehead strong against their foreheads.

As an adamant harder than flint have I made thy forehead: fear them not, neither be dismayed at their looks, though they [be] a rebellious house.

God tells Ezekiel that it will be a tough job to minister to the Jewish people but that He would give him the strength to deal with them.

Ezekiel as a Watchman

As we continue our study, we see God call Ezekiel to be a watchman.

EZEKIEL 3:17

Son of man, I have made thee a watchman unto the house of Israel: therefore hear the word at my mouth, and give them warning from me.

You know what a watchman would do? A watchman, in the days of the Bible, would stand on the wall of the city, because that was the only defense a city had. He would stand on the wall and, particularly at night, he would look out across the horizon to see if anybody was coming. If he saw someone coming, the watchman would either blow the shofar to give the people warning that there was an incoming enemy, or he would somehow start communicating to them that somebody was coming. That's applicable to what God is talking about here. He wants these Jewish people to be forewarned about what is going to happen. He made that statement. He said, "I will give you information about what's coming before I allow it to come."

By the way, we all need to be watchmen. Notice in verse 17 what a watchman does:

> EZEKIEL 3:17
>
> *Son of man, I have made thee a watchman unto the house of Israel: therefore hear the word at my mouth, ...*

That's the first part of being a watchman: hear what God has to say to us. And He says it through His book.

> EZEKIEL 3:17 (continued)
>
> *... and give them warning from me.*

We need to be watchmen today. We need to hear what God's Word is saying and warn the people, particularly in light of the end times in which we are now living.

Ezekiel as a Street Preacher

Did you know that Ezekiel became the first street preacher? God has unique ways in which He performs His ministries through us. Here, He makes Ezekiel a prophet and He makes him dumb, as in unable to speak.

EZEKIEL 3:26-27

And I will make thy tongue cleave to the roof of thy mouth, that thou shalt be dumb, and shalt not be to them a reprover: for they [are] a rebellious house.

But when I speak with thee, I will open thy mouth, and thou shalt say unto them, Thus saith the Lord GOD; ....

Isn't that interesting? For seven-and-a-half years, Ezekiel is going to be a prophet to the people, but he's not going to be able to say anything. Not a thing. His tongue will cleave to the roof of his mouth. The only thing he'll ever say is when God opens it up and he makes a statement. Wow. Man, I've heard about street preachers, but not "dumb" street preachers ("can't talk" type of dumb).

You know what he does? God tells him to lay in the street. He lays in the street on his left side for three hundred and ninety days. He lays on his right side for forty days. In all, Ezekiel lays in the street for a total of four hundred and thirty days.

EZEKIEL 4:5

For I have laid upon thee the years of their iniquity, according to the number of the days, three hundred and ninety days:....

That's on his left side.

EZEKIEL 4:6

And when thou hast accomplished them, lie again on thy right side, and thou shalt bear the iniquity of the house of Judah forty days: ....

Four hundred and thirty days, Ezekiel, with his tongue cleaving to the roof of his mouth, laid in the middle of the street. What kind of a prophet is that?

And then God says, "Hey, Ezekiel, you are probably going to be hungry. I'll tell you what, I'm going to give you something to eat. I'm going to give you eight ounces of meat every day. I'm going to give you a quart of water every day, and I'm going to let you bake your bread." In fact, He gives him the ingredients for the bread. I don't know if you've ever been to a health food store, but they have Ezekiel bread in there made out of the same ingredients. Look at what the ingredients are:

EZEKIEL 4:9

Take thou also thee wheat, and barley, and beans, and lentiles, and millet, and fitches, and put them in one vessel, and make thee bread thereof, ...

Now, I hope they don't bake today's healthy versions the same way that Ezekiel had to bake his loaves. You know how Ezekiel was supposed to bake the bread? I'm not trying to be funny, and I am not trying to be vulgar. God told Ezekiel, "Here's the ingredients, mix them together, and go out there in the middle of the street and take a bowel movement. And then when that human excrement is laying in the street, you put it all together and you bake your bread over that bowel movement that you just took in public." Think I'm making that up? Look at verse 12.

EZEKIEL 4:12

And thou shalt eat it [as] barley cakes, and thou shalt bake it with dung that cometh out of man, in their sight.

Go out in the street and do that. God is making this man a proverb, a prophet, a sign unto His people; and He's got him doing some strange things.

By the way, Ezekiel comes back to the Lord and says, "Lord, don't you remember what you wrote in Deuteronomy? It is not kosher to take a bowel movement in public." (Deuteronomy 23:13) And God said, "That's right, you're correct. OK, you won't use human excrement to bake your bread, you'll use cow manure." I can just hear old Ezekiel's response, "Thanks a lot, God, that's a lot better." Look at verse 15; it is exactly what God says.

EZEKIEL 4:15

Then he said unto me, Lo, I have given thee cow's dung for man's dung and thou shalt prepare thy bread therewith.

God is using this man in every aspect of his life to do what He wants him to do. He wants him to be a prophet to His people.

Three Piles of Ezekiel's Hair

The fifth chapter is strange as well. Not quite as strange as baking your bread over cow manure, but it is strange. Ezekiel has a beard and a head of hair, and God says, "Cut off all your hair. Cut the hair off your head, cut the hair off your face, and put it in three equal piles. In one pile, you take your dagger out and you stab that pile of hair. In the other pile, you take fire and you light that hair and burn it up. In the third pile, you take a little bit out of it, put it in your belt, and throw the rest of it in the air." What in the world? I mean, I've seen those gospel artists who draw a picture while you are standing there, but I've never seen one of them cut off all his hair, divide it into piles, then stab one, burn one, and throw one in the air. God then told him what it was all about.

EZEKIEL 5:12

A third part of thee shall die with the pestilence, and with famine shall they be consumed in the midst of thee:....

That is that hair being burned up.

EZEKIEL 5:12 (continued)

... and a third part shall fall by the sword round about thee;....

That is that third of the hair being stabbed by his dagger.

EZEKIEL 5:12 (continued)

... and I will scatter a third part into all the winds, and I will draw out a sword after them.

That's the third he takes into the Babylonian captivity. God is using this street preacher. Unbelievable.

Go to the twenty-fourth chapter. Ezekiel is a married man. As a priest, he was allowed to be married, but Levitical law imposed certain restrictions as to who he could marry. He had known this young lady from his youth up. Notice what it says is going to happen.

EZEKIEL 24:15-16

Also the word of the LORD came unto me, saying,

Son of man, behold, I take away from thee the desire of thine eyes with a stroke: yet neither shalt thou mourn nor weep, neither shall thy tears run down.

In other words, they pronounced Sheva. "Sheva" in Hebrew is "seven," and for seven days, when a Jewish person's family member or some dear one close to them dies, they rip their clothes off, they mourn, they don't eat. Mourning the death is pronouncing Sheva. Now that is what he is told <u>not</u> to do. God tells him, "The wife of your youth is going to die, but don't you shed a tear."

EZEKIEL 24:17-18

Forbear to cry, make no mourning for the dead, bind the tire of thine head upon thee, and put on thy shoes upon thy feet, and cover not [thy] lips, and eat not the bread of men.

So I spake unto the people in the morning: and at even my wife died; and I did in the morning as I was commanded.

God takes his wife away, but doesn't allow him to mourn her death. Ezekiel is instructed to go back to work like nothing has happened. Ezekiel: unique prophet; unique ministry.

The Valley of Dry Bones

Look at chapter 37 for a moment. Let me show you what God calls Ezekiel to do. He brings him to a valley. I don't think this is simply a vision, but a literal valley that he is taken to.

EZEKIEL 37:1-3

The hand of the Lord was upon me, and carried me out in the spirit of the Lord, and set me down in the midst of the valley which [was] full of bones,

And caused me to pass by them round about: and, behold, [there were] very many in the open valley; and, lo, [they were] very dry.

And he said unto me, Son of man, can these bones live?....

I love his answer. God said to Ezekiel, "Hey, Ezekiel, can these bones live?" Notice what Ezekiel says.

EZEKIEL 37:3 (continued)

...And I answered, O Lord GOD, thou knowest.

In other words, when that professor or that teacher asks you a dumb question you don't know how to answer, just write down the answer, "You know. Why are you asking me a dumb question like this?" I did that in college and it worked one time, that's all. They caught me from then on. But I want you to notice what God tells him to do.

EZEKIEL 37:4

Again he said unto me, Prophesy upon these bones, and say unto them, O ye dry bones, hear the word of the LORD.

God took him to a valley and told him to go out and preach to the dry bones. God said, "Preach to the bones, Ezekiel."

Ezekiel's Consistency in Obedience

I want you to notice something. When God said, "Go to your people, a rebellious people, and speak to them no matter what they say or what they look like"; Ezekiel said, "Yes, sir." When God said, "Lay in the street for four hundred and thirty days on your left and right sides"; Ezekiel said, "Yes, sir." When God said, "Bake your bread over cow manure"; Ezekiel said, "Yes, sir." When God said, "Cut your hair off, stab it, burn it, throw it in the air"; Ezekiel said, "Yes, sir." When God said, "I'm going to take your wife, the love of your life; don't you mourn, you get back to the task"; Ezekiel said, "Yes, sir." When

God said, "Preach to a valley of dry bones"; Ezekiel said, "Yes, sir." How could he do that?

The Four Living Creatures

Go back to the first chapter. We're going to see exactly how Ezekiel could do—without hesitation—whatever God told him to do. It's all contained in the first chapter. Let me tell you right now, I'm going to have difficulty explaining this chapter to you. I do not know all that it is talking about. I don't understand it. I'll show you what I'm talking about in just a moment. I'll give you as much as I can.

Ezekiel is thirty years of age. He has just finished his priestly responsibilities of learning how to operate a Temple through the sacrificial system, the worship service, and all that goes on in a Temple. He is qualified. He's taken out of Jerusalem and taken to Babylon, to the Chebar River. And there, as he is standing on the riverside, look what happens:

EZEKIEL 1:4

And I looked, and, behold, a whirlwind came out of the north, a great cloud, and a fire infolding itself, ...

Now, there's the first problem I have: I don't understand how a fire enfolds itself. I am using a King James Bible, but I'll have to study more. How does a fire enfold itself? All of a sudden Ezekiel looks up in the sky and there is a fire up there, a great cloud and a fire enfolding itself.

EZEKIEL 1:4 (continued)-6

... and a brightness [was] about it, and out of the midst thereof as the colour of amber, out of the midst of the fire.

Also out of the midst thereof [came] the likeness of four living creatures. And this [was] their appearance; they had the likeness of a man.

And every one had four faces, ...

Now he sees four creatures, all of them having four faces.

EZEKIEL 1:6-9

And every one had four faces, and every one had four wings.

And their feet [were] straight feet; and the sole of their feet [was] like the sole of a calf's foot: and they sparkled like the colour of burnished brass.

And [they had] the hands of a man under their wings on their four sides; and they four had their faces and their wings.

Their wings [were] joined one to another; they turned not when they went; they went every one straight forward.

Because I've read about them in the tenth chapter, I can tell you who these four creatures are. They are cherubim. They are one aspect of the angels that were created. You have the seraphim, you have the cherubim, and you have the throne room angels, which are different than the seraphim and the cherubim. But these are cherubim. Chapter 10 talks about that. There were four of them. They each had four wings; two wings extended out and two wings covered their body. Then the four were standing in the shape of a square, because they are forming a throne chariot to bring the glory of the Lord to the earth. Look at these creatures just a moment. We read about their feet, their hands, and underneath their wings.

Verse 10 in the first chapter says these are all male. There are no female angels. Sorry, girls. All these little postcards you send out with these cute little angels just aren't accurate; no, there are going to be a bunch of ugly men who are angels. Actually, I don't know if they will be ugly, but I'm going to show you what the cherubim looked like.

EZEKIEL 1:10

As for the likeness of their faces, they four had the face of a man, and the face of a lion, on the right side: and they four had the face of an ox on the left side; they four also had the face of an eagle.

So, in the front is the face of a man, on the right is the face of a lion, on the left is the face of an ox, and in the back is the face of an eagle.

By the way, I do think I understand what that is talking about. I believe each cherub, with his faces, displays the different aspects of Jesus Christ as He came to earth. In the Bible, the book of Matthew presents Jesus as royalty; the King of kings, and Lord of lords. That, of course, is the face on the right side of the cherub, the face of a lion; king of the animal world. Then the book of Mark presents Him as a servant; thus the ox on the left side, the servant animal. The book of Luke, presents Him as a man, which is the face of the man on the front. And the book of John presents Him as deity, which is the face of an eagle on the back. So, on the right side of the cherub, the lion depicts royalty (Matthew); on the left side, the ox depicts a servant (Mark); in front, man is represented (Luke); and in back, the eagle depicts deity (John).

EZEKIEL 1:11-12

Thus [were] their faces: and their wings [were] stretched upward; two [wings] of every one [were] joined one to another, and two covered their bodies.

And they went every one straight forward: whither the spirit was to go, they went; [and] they turned not when they went.

Described are four cherubim, each standing with two wings out and two wings covering their body. And the two wings out touch the wing tips of two others, forming a perfect square. They don't have to turn their head. Why turn your head? Their four faces now face in all directions. So they just go; they just go ahead. It's amazing. Unbelievable.

Now, let's look at how they move. Here's where I really have the problem.

> EZEKIEL 1:15-16
>
> *Now as I beheld the living creatures, behold one wheel upon the earth by the living creatures, with his four faces.*
>
> *The appearance of the wheels and their work [was] like unto the colour of a beryl: and they four had one likeness: and their appearance and their work [was] as it were a wheel in the middle of a wheel.*

I don't know how to explain it, folks: *"a wheel in the middle of a wheel."* They would go and they would move and this is coming out of the sky. It's coming down to the earth.

How to See the Glory of the Lord

> EZEKIEL 1:24-26
>
> *And when they went, I heard the noise of their wings, like the noise of great waters, as the voice of the Almighty, ...*
>
> *And there was a voice from the firmament that [was] over their heads, when they stood, [and] had let down their wings.*
>
> *And above the firmament that [was] over their heads [was] the likeness of a throne, ...*

There's where I get the idea of a throne chariot coming down.

 EZEKIEL 1:27

And I saw as the colour of amber, as the appearance of fire round about within it, from the appearance of his loins even upward, and from the appearance of his loins even downward, ...

Now look here, folks. I'm trying to illustrate this for you. On this throne chariot, you've got the four cherubim; they are moving, they have a wheel in the middle of a wheel, that's how they move. They sound like rushing water when they are moving, and there's a rainbow over this throne chariot coming down. There is the appearance of a man here from his belly up; and from his belt up there is fire, from his belt down there is fire. He comes to Ezekiel. The text says it was *"the glory of the LORD."* That's who came down to see Ezekiel; the glory of the Lord.

You want to know why Ezekiel could say "Yes, sir"? He saw the glory of the Lord. I want to tell you something: this is a pre-incarnate appearance of Christ. Our problem is that we've not seen the glory of the Lord. If we, literally, see the glory of the Lord, we'll be immediately obedient as well. You say, "Wait a minute, DeYoung. We don't believe in visions." I don't believe in visions either. But I have seen the glory of the Lord. You know what I have seen?

PSALM 19:1

The heavens declare the glory of God; and the firmament sheweth his handywork.

I have seen His creation. When I walk slowly, looking at the majestic colors in the flower gardens, I see the glory of the Lord; how He took a red and a blue and a green, and put them together. That's His glory. He spoke.

When was the last time you looked in the heavens? They tell me Einstein said there are twelve octillion stars in our galaxy, the Milky Way. Do you know how much twelve octillion is? It is a twenty-nine-digit number; the number "twelve" with twenty-seven zeroes behind it. I would have a difficult time writing down such a number, and even more difficulty grasping how very large the number is. Twelve octillion stars. Now listen to this. Astronomers tell us that our galaxy is one of one billion galaxies. Wow!

You know what God did? He almost forgot to make the stars. On the fourth day of creation, in the first chapter of Genesis, He created the sun (the greater light), the moon (the lesser light), and it was as if He was going back to take a rest. Oh, and the stars also. Isn't that great? Three words—"...*the stars also*" (Genesis 1:16). He spreads them across the sky. One billion galaxies times twelve octillion stars. That's a lot of stars. Do you know the smallest star? When we get out to eternity future, you know what we're going to have to do? We're going to have to be really moving to go from the side of one star to the side of another star. Do you know how long it's going to take us, traveling at one hundred and eighty-six thousand miles per second (that's the speed of light, or seven times around the earth in one second)? Traveling at that speed, we'll have to take off and go for one hundred thousand years to get to the other side of that star. And that's a little one. Man, that winds my clock.

Have you ever seen a woodpecker? I love the woodpecker. The Bible says, in II Peter 3, that in the end times there will be those people who deny the coming of the Lord. Not only will they deny His coming, they will also deny creation. They will be willfully ignorant. I have a better translation for that—they will be dumb on purpose. I cannot believe these people. People want to tell me that the woodpecker evolved. Do you know anything about the woodpecker? The woodpecker is a unique creature. Let's just imagine that a blue jay wanted to evolve into a woodpecker, because a woodpecker is more complex than a simple old blue jay.

Now, if a blue jay wanted to be a woodpecker, he would have to figure out in his brain, over thousands of years, how to fly up to a tree and put his claws into the tree. But, there's one problem with a blue jay being a woodpecker. When that blue jay uses his claws to hold onto the tree and pecks with his beak one time, he falls off the tree. You see, the woodpecker is built differently.

The woodpecker's claws are reversed, so when he comes up to the tree, he can sink his claws in.

Now, if the blue jay was going to try and be a woodpecker, he would take his tail and balance himself in a triad. But, he has a very weak tail that would just break right to pieces. The woodpecker, however, has a reinforced tail so that when he lands on the tree, he can position his claws and his tail to form a triad. Man, he's set and ready to go; you can't knock him off that tree. Then he takes his beak and he starts pecking against the tree.

Now, I've got to tell you something else. If a blue jay could hang on to the side of a tree, and if he could properly balance himself, once he began to peck, he would kill himself. The blue jay has a soft membrane in the back of his head; once he started pecking, he would drive his beak through his brain. He dies. But a woodpecker has a very strong membrane, and when he takes that beak and goes peck-peck, he pecks a hole in that wood. You know what he's looking for, don't you? He's looking for a worm in there. He's starving to death, so he goes peck-peck.

And another thing, a blue jay wouldn't even be able to get the worm out, because a blue jay has a short tongue. Not only does the woodpecker have a long tongue (it goes around his head so he can slip both his head and out-stretched tongue into the hole), but the woodpecker has a glue-like substance on the end of his tongue and a hook. So he jabs his head into the hole, grabs that worm, sticks it to his hook, and brings it out. Can't you just imagine a blue jay climbing up, "I've got to get my tongue in there. How am I going to make it sticky?" So he grabs a gob of glue and puts it on his tongue. He puts too much glue on, and he's stuck in the tree.

I'm sorry for being so frivolous. You know, that's what we ought to think about these scientists who are dumb on purpose; scientists who are going to tell me that a blue jay can become a woodpecker.

What about the giraffe with a neck eighteen feet long? Just visualize a giraffe walking along, and he gets thirsty. He sees a body of water and he leans over. Can you imagine having an eighteen-foot-long neck leaning down into the water? You know what would happen? If you didn't have special apparatus inside your neck, all the blood in your body would go right to your head and you'd fall in the water and drown. But that's not the worst part. If the giraffe does lean down and everything settles, then all of a sudden he sees a lion coming and he quickly straightens back up, guess what happens then? All the blood from his brain goes down, and he dies right there on the spot. God has specially put together a giraffe with an apparatus that lets the blood flow and return.

Ever looked closely at an egg? Judy boiled an egg one morning, and when she peeled it, it wasn't totally symmetric. It had a little spot on it. You know what that little spot was? It was an oxygen bag. That egg shell has ten-thousand little holes in it to get oxygen in so that the egg, if it is fertilized, can become a chick. It has exactly eighteen days of oxygen supply and the chick develops a beak so he can peck out of that shell.

That's the glory of God all around us. We can see His glory like Ezekiel saw it. And when He says to do something, our response should be "Yes, sir. God, I see Your glory." Don't you want to see His glory? Don't you want to serve Him? He's coming.

The Fall of Lucifer and His Angels

We are going to study how Lucifer, the most prominent of all the cherubs, fell from that position of prominence and became the ruler of this world. That is going to be the beginning of our study. We are going to look at where angels came from when they were created, what part they play in end-time prophecy, and what the next great significant event with an angel will be—an event that will be used to cause the world to fall under the dominion of Satan himself.

Walk-Through of Future Events

I want you to picture three pillars lined up in a row. They represent the three main future events on God's calendar.

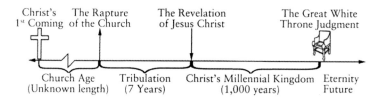

Remember, six thousand years ago Jesus Christ created the heavens, the earth, and all that is in them. We move forward four thousand years, and Jesus Christ is born, dies, is buried, and resurrects. After two thousand more years, we come to today, where we are quickly approaching what the first pillar represents: the next main event on God's calendar of activities, the rapture of the church. After that will be a seven-year period of time, the Tribulation, a terrible time of judgment. Following the Tribulation, we get to the second pillar: the Revelation of Jesus Christ, when He comes back to earth, placing His feet on the Mount of Olives. At that point in time, there will be the conclusion of the campaign of Armageddon, which actually starts in Jerusalem and culminates in the Jezreel Valley. Then Jesus will restructure the city of Jerusalem and will set up His kingdom, a kingdom from which He will rule and reign for a thousand years. There will be a Temple that is operating out of the city of Jerusalem; called Messiah's Temple, it is described in the book of Ezekiel. At the conclusion of those thousand years, we reach the third pillar, which represents the final main event, the retribution in our walk through eschatology: the Great White Throne Judgment. Jesus Christ will be the Judge, sentencing those who have rejected Him to the lake of fire, which is the second death. Then eternity future— new heaven, new earth, and new Jerusalem.

A key player in all of these activities, up until the end of the Millennial Kingdom, is Lucifer, the most prominent creature ever created by God. We see the account of this in Ezekiel 28. So let's look at that chapter and glean some information from it, and we will go to other locations to put it all together.

By the way, if you remember the outline that I gave you, I told you that the book of Ezekiel was basically divided into two parts. The first thirty-two chapters are a message of retribution. Ezekiel would have the message going forth through different means as God used him: laying in the street; baking his bread over cow manure; cutting his hair off of his head; and not being mournful and pronouncing Sheva at the time of the death of his wife, instead just going ahead and serving the Lord. Then I said that, within the framework of those thirty-two chapters, the first twenty-four chapters deal with judgment against Israel, the Jewish people; and chapters 25 through 32 were judgment against the neighbors of the Jewish people. It is interesting to study those judgments. We will not really dig into that, but when I tell you who the people are, you can go back and you'll be able to better understand and have a world view.

You know, every one of us has a world view. A world view is how you look at current events unfolding and why they may be happening. Most of us are fed, or at least indoctrinated for, our world view by the media of this world. We listen to what they say, we assimilate their (basically) false teaching, and then we apply that to understand why events are unfolding. A true Christian world view has to, first, be based upon a person's knowledge of the Word of God, and, second, be based upon the scenario prophetically laid out in God's Word.

When I had the privilege and opportunity of speaking at the Pentagon, I spoke to a group of generals. And I was really overjoyed about that because, though I was in the service, I was not an officer. I was in the Air Force for three years, nine months, twenty-seven days, ten hours, fifteen minutes, and thirty seconds. I loved every minute of that. But I was an enlisted man. And there I was, standing as an enlisted man in front of all those generals. I was going to speak on prophecy, of course. That's basically what I do when I go someplace. So, as I stood there and looked at them, I said, "Gentlemen, today you are going to make decisions that will affect tomorrow. Today, you'd better understand what is going to happen tomorrow."

I think that's appropriate for all of us, no matter what our age may be and no matter what our position in life. All of us are going to make decisions today that will affect tomorrow. How much better informed those decisions would be if—today—we know what is going to happen tomorrow. The best way we can understand what is going to happen tomorrow, is by developing a proper world view based upon God's Word and the prophetic scenario laid out in it. Such understanding will help us to grasp what is happening in these nations, especially in the Middle East. For example, why is there an attempt to overthrow the Lebanese government, which is basically anti-Syrian? Why had the world put so much pressure on Syria to withdraw from Lebanon? That's one example. There are events occurring all around the world, and there is a reason for those events happening as it relates to God's prophetic scenario for the end times. So it behooves us to study these things and have a handle on why things are happening. Our study will also enhance our urgency for the return of the Lord Jesus Christ. That plays key into how we then live out our Christian experience.

Identity of the Prince of Tyre

I told you it was key to have an outline to get the overall big picture of a book that you may be studying, and this is the twenty-eighth chapter. So thus, as I look at my outline, it indicates we are looking at a judgment pronounced against one of the enemies of Israel, one of their neighbors. Now as we start to read this chapter, we see that he is talking about the king or the prince of Tyre.

Let me tell you who Tyre is. Tyre, in scriptural, Biblical times, would be modern-day Lebanon. Modern-day Lebanon is very active as it relates to Israel. It was out of southern Lebanon that Hezbollah, organized by the Iranian Revolutionary Guard, emerged in 1982. Ayatollah Khomeini placed this militant group in southern Lebanon. They were the ones responsible for blowing up the Marine barracks, an attack that killed over two hundred and eighty U.S. Marine soldiers. They are the ones who entered into Israel in 2006 and started a cross-border war that lasted for thirty-four days, ending in the result that Israel, according to the perception of the Islamic-Arab world, was defeated; the invincible Israeli Defense Force was brought to their knees. And I happen to agree with that perception of the Arab world.

Perception is key in the Middle East. It's not whether Israel has a nuclear weapon or not, it's whether the Islamic-Arab world believes they have a nuclear weapon. They don't have to have one to pose a threat that they do. And nobody knows. So if somebody ever tells you that they know for sure Israel has a nuclear weapon, you just walk away from that individual because he or she is a liar. They do not know. Not one single person knows, unless they happen to be the Prime Minister of Israel or somebody along that line. If a person said that there was a nuclear weapon, in telling that, the Mossad (national intelligence agency of Israel) would take him out in a heartbeat. So don't let any prophecy teacher tell you he knows for sure that Israel has nuclear weapons. Now, I happen to think that they do. Don't quote me as saying they do, but I think they do. The perception, according to the Islamic world, is that they have one. And that is what is important— perception.

The Israeli government doesn't do PR to America, to the European Union, or to any place in the world. I have known some of the key players in the Israeli government, and one of them was Morty Delinsky. He was the director of the government press office. He gave credentials to all journalists coming into the land. He was the spokesperson to talk to the world. Morty was an orthodox Jew who God allowed me to develop a great relationship with, and he told me, "I don't care what America thinks about Israel. What I care about is what these Islamic-Arab countries think about Israel. I want them to perceive that if they touch us, we are going to cut their heads off." That was the perception, until 2006 in the Hezbollah Conflict.

Tyre played a key role in Lebanon, which is right here at the beginning of chapter 28, and this is a prophecy against them. I'm not going to go into that, but I also wanted to let you know that when we come to verse 13 in chapter 28, it changes from talking about a judgment against Tyre (or modern-day Lebanon), and instead talks about Lucifer, that prominent cherub whom God created early on.

> EZEKIEL 28:13
> *Thou hast been in Eden the garden of God;*
> ....

Now this is focal. The king of Tyre was never in the Garden of Eden. So at verse 13, this particular prophecy changes in focus. Look at the last phrase in verse 13:

> EZEKIEL 28:13
> *... in the day that thou wast created.*

So it is that this individual, Lucifer, the most prominent of all creatures, was in the Garden of Eden when created.

EZEKIEL 28:14

Thou [art] the anointed cherub that covereth; and I have set thee [so]: thou wast upon the holy mountain of God; ....

Now it said he was in the Garden of Eden. I draw your attention to the fact that it says he was in the holy mountain of God, wherever that location was. Go to the ninth chapter in the book of Daniel and let me show you a definition, or an interpretation of that phrase, "the holy mountain of God." This is Daniel's prayer after he realized where he was in God's time.

DANIEL 9:16

O Lord, according to all thy righteousness, I beseech thee, let thine anger and thy fury be turned away from thy city Jerusalem, thy holy mountain: ....

So he is defining what the holy mountain of God is, it is the city of Jerusalem.

DANIEL 9:20

And whiles I [was] speaking, and praying, and confessing my sin and the sin of my people Israel, and presenting my supplication before the LORD my God for the holy mountain of my God;

He's talking about the city of Jerusalem. That phrase, the "holy mountain of God," is used eighteen times in the Old Testament. This is talking about the city of Jerusalem. And that gives me the first hint. I talked about letting you know where the Garden of Eden was originally located, where it is today, and where it shall be in the future. So, Lucifer is in the holy mountain of God, synonymous with the Garden of Eden. The holy mountain of God is used twice in chapter 28, and it is used sixteen other times throughout the Old Testament. Every other time that it is used, in its context, it is talking about the Temple Mount in the city of Jerusalem. I tell you that the original location of the Garden of Eden is the Temple Mount in the city of Jerusalem. Under that gold-domed building—that "Dome of the Rock"—is what the Jewish people call the foundation stone.

This year (September 28, 2011 – September 16, 2012) is the year 5772 in the Jewish calendar. In other words, they believe creation took place five thousand seven hundred and seventy-two years ago. For those five thousand seven hundred and seventy-two years, they have believed that the Temple Mount, Mount Moriah—where Abraham offered Isaac (Genesis 22), which King David purchased from Araunah the Jebusite (II Samuel 24), and where Solomon built that Temple (II Chronicles 3:1)—is the original site of the Garden of Eden.

The Fall of Lucifer

I just simply point out to you Lucifer, this prominent cherub that God placed in his position. Look again at these verses:

EZEKIEL 28:14-15

Thou [art] the anointed cherub that covereth; and I have set thee [so]: thou wast upon the holy mountain of God; thou hast walked up and down in the midst of the stones of fire.

Thou [wast] perfect in thy ways from the day that thou wast created, ...

By the way, that would not be applicable for the king of Tyre. So again, I am pointing out that this chapter is not only dealing with the king of Tyre, but with Lucifer. He was perfect in his ways until iniquity was found in him. Thus he is going to fall.

Why is he going to fall? In Isaiah 14 we find out his name and we find out why he fell. Angels are created, or were created, with a free will, as is man. Every angel had an opportunity to exercise his free will. You and I have a free will. The difference between human free will and angelic free will is that we can continue to change our minds as we exercise our free will. But an angel has only one opportunity to exercise his free will, and at that point, he is locked in for eternity. So, there is no redemption for an angel once he has exercised his free will and chosen who he is going to go with.

I'll prove that he has a free will. Look at Isaiah 14:

ISAIAH 14:12-13

How art thou fallen from heaven, O Lucifer, son of the morning! [how] art thou cut down to the ground, which didst weaken the nations!

> *For thou hast said in thine heart, I will*
> *ascend into heaven, I will exalt my throne above*
> *the stars of God: I will sit also upon the mount*
> *of the congregation, in the sides of the north:*

By the way, in Psalm 48:2, that is a description of the city of Jerusalem. So, Lucifer, who is going to become Satan, is making the statement, "not only will I go into the heavens, not only will I be equal with God, not only will I do this, but I will be worshipped in Jerusalem." Keep that thought in mind as we go through our study.

ISAIAH 14:14

> *I will ascend above the heights of the*
> *clouds; I will be like the most High.*

When Lucifer makes that statement, the battle of the ages begins. We are going to see when Lucifer probably would have fallen and taken one-third of the angels with him, angels who would also determine that they were going to exercise their free will and rebel against God. At that point in time, what had been a theocracy, through the first three chapters of the book of Genesis, became a Satan-ocracy; and a theocracy will not be re-implemented until the last three chapters of the Bible.

So you have, in Genesis 1, 2, and 3, a theocracy—God controlling the government governing humankind. In the last three chapters of the Bible, in Revelation 20, 21, and 22, a theocracy is once again implemented. In Revelation 20, verses 4, 5, and 6, the Millennial Kingdom is established, and that will be a theocratic government. But all in between Genesis 3 and Revelation 20, Satan is the ruler of this world. He is the king in charge under the sovereignty of almighty God. God allows him to be that.

Do you remember when Jesus was tempted? What did Satan say to him? "All you have to do is 'this' and I will give you the kingdoms of the world." Now he could not have offered the kingdoms of the world to Jesus if he didn't have the kingdoms of the world. He is the one controlling this world today. It is a Satan-ocracy that is in place at this point in time. Well, I take you to that bit of information in the book of Isaiah for the purpose of understanding that he can exercise his free will.

Where did Angels Come From?

Speaking of angels, I think we need to spend a few moments understanding how angels came into existence and some of the activities they are going to be involved in. The Bible, in the first chapter of Genesis, gives us the information about the six days of creation. Chapter 2 goes into detail about some of the events that took place in that creation week. In both chapters 1 and 2, we see no statement as to when angels were created.

There are those who teach, using all kinds of charts, and make the statement that angels are prehistoric creatures. "Evil angels fell in prehistoric times." Now, as soon as these teachers use the word "prehistoric," you should turn off the television. It shows their ignorance.

"Prehistoric" is an oxymoron that doesn't mean anything. How can you have something before history? I mean, that's stupidity. Nothing except God was before history. Do you know what history is? His story. You know when it was started? In the beginning, God. That's when history started. From Genesis 1:1, it continues all the way over to Revelation 21, when we have new heavens, new earth, no more time, no more night, no more history. Eternity future.

So there is nothing prehistoric. If people don't understand how to explain what the Bible says, they just throw everything over in prehistoric times. They say, "Dinosaurs were created in prehistoric times. They are prehistoric animals." Baloney! They were created on the sixth day of creation when He created all creeping things upon the earth, before He created man.

The Bible tells us every single thing about how we came into existence, but it does not mention when angels specifically were created. How, then, do you come to a conclusion and an understanding of when they were created? Well, just like you would, for example, if you are trying to develop your doctrine on the Trinity. There is no single verse that says "this explains the Trinity." What do you do? You assimilate a bunch of passages that have a relationship to the Trinity and then, as you assimilate these, you come to a conclusion. That's how you have to come to a conclusion on when angels were created.

Go to the book of Job. We'll come back to Ezekiel, but let's look and see if we can come to some understanding of when angels were created. The book of Job, you might well know, is probably the oldest book in the Bible, and most likely it's dealing with a man who lived in the vicinity of the city of Jerusalem. He describes dinosaurs, which—until about a hundred and fifty years ago, when that word was created by some English professor—were called large lizards. But now we call them dinosaurs, because we are so well educated. They were not called dinosaurs early on, they were called large lizards. In fact, there are some dinosaurs that are still alive today.

As a herpetologist by hobby, I can tell you that there are still dinosaurs on earth. There are a bunch of them out in the Everglades; they call them alligators. That's what a dinosaur was. Those were not created in prehistoric times, but on the sixth day of creation. By the way, I tell you that because you can look over in Job 40 sometime and see him describing a dinosaur with a tail like a big log gulping up the Jordan River down there in Jericho. It's an exciting book, so, let me show you about angels.

Look at Job 38. Let me just set the scene for you. Old Job is really uptight. He's lost his wife, he's lost his kids, he's lost his health, he's lost his wealth—he's lost everything. And some of his "good friends" come to him and say, "Why don't you just denounce God and die?" Well, you know he's not going to do that. But about that time, the Lord comes along and is going to have a conversation with Job. He speaks rather loudly so those neighbors, or so-called friends, of Job can overhear Him. Here's what God says:

JOB 38:1-2

Then the LORD answered Job out of the whirlwind, and said,

Who [is] this that darkeneth counsel by words without knowledge?

Now Job is starting to question what God did. Here's what God says in the next verse:

JOB 38:3

Gird up now thy loins like a man; for I will demand of thee, and answer thou me.

"Be a man, Job. Stand up and ask your question. But before you do, let me ask you a question." Look at the question God asked:

JOB 38:4

Where wast thou when I laid the foundations of the earth?....

"You've got a problem? Where were you when I laid the foundations of the earth?"

JOB 38:4 (continued)-5

... declare, if thou hast understanding.

Who hath laid the measures thereof, if thou knowest? or who hath stretched the line upon it?

"Have you ever measured the earth or the foundations of the earth, Job?"

JOB 38:6

Whereupon are the foundations thereof fastened? ....

"How are they fastened to the earth, Job? You think you have a problem? Tell me; answer these questions."

JOB 38:6 (continued)-7

... or who laid the corner stone thereof;
When the morning stars sang together, and all the sons of God shouted for joy?

That gives us the main clue as to when God created angels. Read verse 4 and verse 7 together. Notice this: "*Where wast thou when I laid the foundations of the earth?*" Now go to verse 7, "*When the morning stars sang together, and all the sons of God shouted for joy?*" Whenever God created the earth, the angels shouted for joy.

Now, with that information, let's go back to Genesis 1. I want to show you the time when God created angels.

GENESIS 1:1

In the beginning God created the heaven and the earth.

What is not said is that He created the heavens, the habitation for angels, and before He created the earth,

He created angels. How do I know that? Job 38:7 says they *"shouted for joy"* when He created the earth. I don't know what they said exactly, but they shouted for joy. So, in Genesis 1:1, between *"In the beginning God created the heaven"* and *"and the earth,"* God brought angels into existence. They were there before the earth was created and they were all good angels. How do I know that? Let me show you what God says.

GENESIS 1:31

And God saw every thing that he had made, and, behold, [it was] very good. ....

I love the Hebrew flavor of it—abundantly excellent. Don't you like that? God saw everything he created and it was abundantly excellent.

By the way, that destroys a so-called gap between Genesis 1:1 and 1:2. There is no gap. There is no period of time. These were six 24-hour days, and no period between Genesis 1:1 and Genesis 1:2. How do I know? God said, "Everything I created was excellent; abundantly excellent; very good." So there was no destructive period of time, as some so-called Christian scholars are trying to tell us. Be careful; be very careful of what you study. Keep attuned to the Word of God.

All angels were good angels. They were not created in prehistoric times. Demonic creatures, which are fallen angels possessing a human body, were not in existence before Genesis 1:1.

The Fall of One-third of the Angels

In the six days of creation, they did not fall. But when did the angels fall? I am a little bit unknowledgeable of when, but let me just give you a time frame. Go to Genesis 3:1. Between the sixth day of creation and the time that God is going to have an opportunity to communicate with Adam and Eve in the Garden of Eden, who comes along?

> GENESIS 3:1
>
> *Now the serpent was more subtil than any beast of the field which the LORD God had made.*
> ....

Who is the serpent? Well, Revelation 12:9 says, *"that old serpent, called the Devil."* Satan, that's who the serpent is. It's Satan in the form of a serpent, whatever that serpent may have looked like. Was it like a rattlesnake crawling down? I don't know. It was made then to crawl upon the face of the earth after this. But Satan, in the form of a serpent, appears sometime between Genesis 1:31 and Genesis 3:1. How long a period of time is that? I am not very sure. But, I don't think it was too long. Why? Because in chapter 4, Cain and Abel come into existence and God told them, in chapter 1, to be fruitful and multiply and fill the earth. So it is early on in their existence. That's when Lucifer, the most prominent angel, was above all of creation, in the Garden of Eden (Ezekiel 28:13-14).

Let me show you why he got uptight.

GENESIS 1:28

And God blessed them, and God said unto them, Be fruitful, and multiply, and replenish the earth, and subdue it: and have dominion over the fish of the sea, and over the fowl of the air, and over every living thing that moveth upon the earth.

God gave man dominion. That most prominent of cherubs, Lucifer, possibly said—*or for sure must have thought!*—"I don't like that. I was in charge of creation, now he's given it to man. I will rise above God in the heavens." And he fell. Lucifer became Satan sometime after the sixth day of creation, early on in the existence of humankind. What does he do? He has presence into the third heaven.

There are three heavens. How do I know that? Well, I know there's a first heaven because I can see it out there, where the sun and the clouds are today. That's the first heaven. The second heaven, I saw last night, where the stars and the galaxies are. There's a third heaven. How do I know that? The apostle Paul said in the twelfth chapter of Second Corinthians, "I knew a man fourteen years ago who went to the third heaven." Now I think he's talking about himself. I don't think he meant somebody else. I think God translated him into the third heaven and then physically brought him back; he went up there physically and saw it. Whether you want to agree with that doesn't matter (if you want to be wrong, it's all right with me!), but I think that's where he went. That's where God is and that's where the angels were. Their habitation was the third heaven, in the presence of God. At that point, whatever the time of their fall, the evil angels were thrown out of the third heaven, except for one of them—Lucifer. Satan is the only evil angel who has access to the third heaven. How do I know? Take a look at this Scripture passage:

> REVELATION 12:10
>
> *... for the accuser of our brethren ..., which accused them before our God day and night.*

Satan can go to the throne of God day and night to accuse us who have trusted Jesus Christ as Lord and Savior. He has access to do that. But, basically, his domain is the first and second heavens. How do I know that? I read the Bible.

Let me show you what the sixth chapter of Ephesians says.

> EPHESIANS 6:11
>
> *Put on the whole armour of God, ...*

Why are we supposed to do that? The verse continues.

> EPHESIANS 6:11 (continued)-12
>
> *... that ye may be able to stand against the wiles of the devil.*
>
> *For we wrestle not against flesh and blood, but against principalities, against powers,*

*against the rulers of the darkness of this world,
against spiritual wickedness in high [places].*

"High places" can be translated "heavenlies," as well. On a daily basis, old Satan is right above us in the first and second heavens, and he is there to dispatch evil angels.

Unidentified Flying Objects

I believe in UFOs—unidentified flying objects. Study the ninth chapter of the book of Revelation, where it says alien creatures are going to come out of heaven and attack the earth. Aliens. Creatures that are not normal. You know what they look like? They call them locusts, but these are not like any locusts you know. They have the face of a man, the hair of a woman, the teeth of a lion, the breastplate of a horse running to battle, and a tail like a scorpion, to sting and torment. I've never seen a locust that looked like that. That's an alien creature, and it invades the earth. It's a UFO.

I believe they are active today. We have more sightings of UFOs than you can just throw out the window. I don't believe they are creatures from another planet. I believe they are evil angels taking on the form of whatever we have seen out there. You know why it's going on? Satan has a plan. You know what that plan is? He's going to have to explain the rapture. Because when the rapture takes place, what's the world going to say? "What happened to all those people?" Why do you think we are being inundated with television programs and movies from Hollywood about extra-terrestrial creatures? Our children are being programmed. Harry Potter is a satanic book. (Don't you wish I'd say what I actually believe?) I want to tell you this, they are going to have to explain it away and so the world is being conditioned to accept the explanation that alien creatures have abducted people. That's in the tenth chapter of Daniel.

You want to know why a man in Germany killed six million people because they were guilty of one thing? And do you want to know what they were guilty of? They were "guilty" of being Jewish. You know why a man named Adolf Hitler killed them? Hitler killed the Jews because an evil angel possessed him. Evil angels are dispatched by Satan (II Corinthians 11). What? Don't you know? Satan takes on the form of an angel of light. And some of his "ministers of righteousness" are demonically controlled creatures or religious figures. In Daniel 10: "the prince of Persia," "the prince of Greece." You know what a prince is? In this situation, it's another title for the evil angels. They come and take control of human bodies.

A man named Yasser Arafat walked into a graduation of a group of 13-year-old Palestinian girls. They performed a military parade march, to honor him. Then he got up and he addressed those 13-year-old impressionable young ladies. He said, "I want to tell you about a young lady," and he talked about a female suicide bomber who walked onto a bus on the road between Haifa and Tel Aviv. She did not blow herself into eternity, but she took off her bomb and blew up the bus. Twenty-one people were killed. As she ran from the wreckage, she saw that a baby had been thrown out of the bus, and it was lying on the road, still alive. She ran down there and grabbed up this living baby, then ran back to the burning bus and threw the baby into the bus. Yassar Arafat said, "That's what I want you girls to emulate. She was a heroine." What made a man do that? Satan dispatching evil angels. And he is in that sphere just above us in the first heaven, dispatching evil angels. The most prominent to be dispatched is going to be that one who comes to a male human body. The Bible says in Revelation 13:2, Satan energizes the person who will be the Antichrist with an evil angel, gives him his power, his seat of authority. I believe the Antichrist is alive and well on planet Earth today. He will come to prominence only after the rapture.

The book of Second Thessalonians says the rapture must happen. We depart from this place, going to another place. That's what the Greek word "apostasia" means. Second Thessalonians 2:3 is not talking about a falling away from doctrine. If it were, the Antichrist would have appeared in the first century of the church. Paul was sending Titus and Timothy to these first century churches to build them up in the faith because of apostasy or a falling away. However, the word used in the Greek, in II Thessalonians 2:3, means to depart from one place and go to another. That's what we do at the rapture. The Antichrist cannot appear until we depart from one place and go to another. Then the Antichrist comes on the scene and Satan energizes him, the way Ezekiel told us about it twenty-five hundred years ago. We are here at that time in history. The only event that must occur before the Antichrist appears is the rapture of the church. When that happens, we Christians will be out of here—called up to be with Christ.

Dry Bones and Two Sticks

We are going to study the beginnings of this new series of messages that God gives to Ezekiel. You might remember in the first half of the book of Ezekiel, there is a message of retribution that is being given by Ezekiel to those of the Jewish people who are God's people (chapters 1 through 24), and then to the enemies of the Jewish people (chapters 25 through 32). That message of retribution is given and Ezekiel does that through his street preaching, his different unique acts that he does as it relates to the ministry that God has given him. In fact, he did it with his tongue cleaving to the roof of his mouth; unable to speak, because that was God's plan for using Ezekiel.

In the thirty-third chapter of Ezekiel, God makes the prophet Ezekiel a watchman again. He did that first in the third chapter, but now he's going to recommission him to be a watchman (verse 2), and indeed, it's the same principle. He says, "Hear the words from My mouth and warn the people." That is exactly the message that Ezekiel is going to give forth. He will be a watchman.

EZEKIEL 33:7

So thou, O son of man, I have set thee a watchman unto the house of Israel; therefore thou shalt hear the word at my mouth, and warn them from me.

Now notice what He says, "*I have set thee (Ezekiel) a watchman unto the house of Israel.*" This is a message that is going to Israel. We'll look at that point in just a few moments.

In verse 21, there was one that escaped from Jerusalem as the destruction was taking place. On that same day, in 586 B.C., Nebuchadnezzar brought his Babylonian forces into Jerusalem. The last chapter of Second Chronicles (chapter 36) gives all the details on how he destroyed the city. There were many enemies who came to watch that destruction take place. Finally, Nebuchadnezzar said, "Who would like to burn down the Temple?" Everybody raised their hands and they had to cast lots. One of the reasons that they are going to be wiped out as if they had never existed, as Sodom and Gomorrah were, is because they burned down the Temple in 586 B.C., on this day, the ninth day of the Jewish month of Av.

The one who escaped from Jerusalem, having watched all that took place, gets into Tel Aviv. He goes to where Ezekiel is.

EZEKIEL 33:22

Now the hand of the LORD was upon me in the evening, afore he that was escaped came; and had opened my mouth, until he came to me in the morning; and my mouth was opened, and I was no more dumb.

Not dumb as in "stupid"; dumb as in "can't talk." So he was given back his tongue. He was able, now, to go forth to give this new message.

The Valley of Dry Bones

The new message is going to be a message of restoration. The first message was a message of retribution, or judgment. The new message is a message of restoration. Now go to chapter 37 and let's notice where God is going to take Ezekiel in this unique ministry that He gave him.

God takes Ezekiel out to a valley of dry bones. The dry bones are in the valley, and Ezekiel stands there looking at them. God asked him, in verse 3, "Can the bones live again?" Ezekiel said to the Lord, "Well, thou knowest." And then, without missing a beat, God tells him that he must prophesy upon these bones. In other words, preach to the bones. Ezekiel started to preach and the bones started to come together—the foot bone to the ankle bone, the ankle bone to the leg bone, the leg bone to the hip bone, the hip bone to the back bone, the back bone to the shoulder bone, the shoulder bone to the neck bone, the neck bone to the head bone—and all the bones came together. Ezekiel said, "Boy, that's pretty good preaching." God said, "Preach on, Ezekiel, preach some more now to the sky." Zoom! Skin comes flying and covers these bones. God said, "Preach again, this time to the wind." He preached to the wind and the wind came out and filled these flesh-covered bones and they stood up like a mighty army. Now, that's the text, just embellished a bit.

EZEKIEL 37:7-8

> *So I prophesied as I was commanded: and as I prophesied, there was a noise, and behold a shaking, and the bones came together, bone to his bone.*
>
> *And when I beheld, lo, the sinews and the flesh came up upon them, and the skin covered them above: but [there was] no breath in them.*

God now tells him to preach again; this time, prophesy unto the wind.

EZEKIEL 37:10

> *So I prophesied as he commanded me, and the breath came into them, and they lived, and stood up upon their feet, an exceeding great army.*

This is a three-part prophecy, using the literary technique of apocalyptic literature. Remember I mentioned apocalyptic literature from the Greek word "apocalypses." Apocalyptic means telling the future; prophecy foretelling what is going to happen. It is a way of using a symbol to communicate an absolute truth. It is not an allegory; it is not a fairy tale. It is God using this technique of apocalyptic literature, and He does it in four books: Ezekiel, Daniel, Zechariah, and Revelation. Those are all apocalyptic literature. They all use symbols. You might remember in the book of

Revelation: "as it were a star fell out," or "as it were the Antichrist was wounded to the death," or "as it were *'this happened.'"* That phrase, "as it were, " is used fifty-two times in the book of Revelation and it is simply introducing an apocalyptic phrase that has to be interpreted. It talked about the ten horns coming up out of the sea, a beast coming out of the sea, and it talked about a serpent. That's all apocalyptic literature. But what apocalyptic literature does is it interprets itself. In order to understand what apocalyptic literature is talking about, you simply keep reading.

We are reading about a three-part prophecy here: the bones coming together; the flesh covering the bones; and those flesh-covered bones standing up like a mighty army. What is he speaking about? Look at the next verse for God's interpretation.

EZEKIEL 37:11

Then he said unto me, Son of man, these bones are the whole house of Israel: ....

What he is talking about here is that the whole house of Israel will be regathered—those are the bones coming together. They will be restored—that's the flesh coming on the bones. They will be regenerated—that's the breath of life being breathed into them.

We have seen two-thirds of this three-part prophecy in the process, or almost completely fulfilled. Since the late 1800's, when the first Zionist Congress was held in Basel, Switzerland, people have come into the land from out of one hundred and eight nations of the world. They have come into the land from the four corners of the earth. Jewish people are making Aliyah.

Aliyah is the Jewish people coming back to the land. The word literally means "go up to Jerusalem." Every pilgrim feast day—Passover, Pentecost, and Tabernacles—the Jews are responsible for going back to Jerusalem to the Temple Mount area. Now when the Temple was standing, it was stricter. Today, though, many Jews still make their way back on the pilgrim feast days. By the way, many Christians come to the Feast of Tabernacles every year in Jerusalem. Thousands and thousands of Christians come in because the Bible tells us in Zechariah 14, during the Millennial Kingdom in the future, we are all going to go to Jerusalem once a year for the Feast of Tabernacles. So, today, these Christians are coming in anticipation of that. What we are talking about here is, out of one hundred and eight nations of the world, God gathering these people and bringing them back into the land. That's the regathering.

The restoration—the flesh being put on these bones that have come together—was the establishment of the Jewish state of Israel on May 15, 1948. For the first time in history, a people scattered and separated from each other for two thousand years came back together and reformed their nation in the homeland of their forefathers. That is the only time in history that has ever happened. They came back into the land to do that. God has been working in the hearts and lives of these people to bring them back in the land. There is a desire in a Jewish heart to go back to his homeland. Many of them will resist because of their financial situation, but ultimately, they will end up going back to the land of Israel as a safe haven during the Tribulation period.

The Promise of the Land

Go back to chapter 34 and let me show you why the Jewish people will be going back into the land. God makes some very interesting statements.

> EZEKIEL 34:11-16
>
> *For thus saith the Lord GOD; Behold, I, [even] I, will both search my sheep, and seek them out.*
>
> *... so will I seek out my sheep, and will deliver them out of all places where they have been scattered in the cloudy and dark day.*
>
> *And I will bring them out from the people, and gather them from the countries, and will bring them to their own land, ...*
>
> *I will feed them in a good pasture, and upon the high mountains of Israel shall their fold be: ....*
>
> *I will feed my flock, and I will cause them to lie down, saith the Lord GOD.*
>
> *I will seek that which was lost, and bring again that which was driven away, ...*

Now, you'll notice as you've read just those few verses, they continually repeat a certain phrase, the two words "I will." God is telling Ezekiel, "I will find those

Jews wherever they have been scattered. I will search out every nook and corner of the world. I will find them, I will gather them in, I will bring them into the land, I will feed them like a good shepherd feeds his flock in the land. I will." In fact, if you read from verses 11 to 31, you will see that God makes that statement and repeats it eighteen times. Listen to me, folks. If God says something once to me, I believe it, and that settles it for me. If He says it eighteen times, we had all better pay close attention to what He is saying. "I will find my people where they have been scattered."

When were they scattered? In 70 A.D., General Titus of the Roman Army, who had been bivouacked on the Mount of Olives, came across the Kidron Valley, went into the Temple complex, devastated the Temple, destroyed the city, and dispersed the Jews to the four corners of the earth. Jesus Christ had given a prophecy in the Olivet Discourse that that would happen: Not a stone standing upon a stone would remain. Almost forty years to the day after Jesus Christ made that prophecy in Matthew 24:2, it was fulfilled. The Jews were scattered to the four corners of the earth.

In Deuteronomy 28, Moses tells the Jewish people, "If you don't obey God, God will disperse you to the four corners of the earth." At that time, there had already been two Diasporas; two dispersions of the Jewish people. The first departure is recorded in Genesis, when they left to go down to Egypt. Jacob took his family of seventy people out of the Promised Land, seeking relief from the famine. Then four hundred and thirty years later, Moses brought them back to the edge of the land, and Joshua literally returned them to the land, taking them across the Jordan River. That was the first departure and the first return.

The second departure was in the time of Ezekiel, when they were taken out of the land, into Babylonian captivity. This time they went east to Babylon, instead of south to Egypt. Then seventy years later, God used a man named Zerubbabel to bring the children of Israel back into the land.

Now the third Diaspora is talked about, when they will be dispersed to the four corners of the earth and the Temple devastated. This occurred on the day of Tisha B'Av in 70 A.D. They were dispersed to the four corners of the earth, fulfilling Deuteronomy 28, the prophecy that Moses gave to the Jewish people.

By the way, there is a monument to the fulfillment of that prophecy. In the city of Rome, the Arch of Titus stands in the Coliseum area. You can go and see it. It's probably the only remaining artifact in Rome that is just about exactly like it was when it was built. The monument was erected in 82 A.D. by General Titus's brother, Roman Emperor Domitian (their father was Roman Emperor Vespasian), in honor of his brother's activities in the city of Jerusalem: destruction of the city, devastation of the Temple, and dispersion of the Jews to the four corners of the earth. When they were dispersed this time, God makes this statement through the prophet Ezekiel, in a message of restoration, "I will find them wherever they are scattered. I will gather them together. I will bring them into the land. I will feed them like a good shepherd feeds his flock."

Thirty-five times in chapter 36, Ezekiel is told to write to the land, to deal with the land. So, he is dealing with the land of Israel.

EZEKIEL 36:6

Prophesy therefore concerning the land of Israel, and say unto the mountains, and to the hills, to the rivers, and to the valleys, Thus saith the Lord GOD; ....

EZEKIEL 36:8

But ye, O mountains of Israel, ye shall shoot forth your branches, and yield your fruit to my people of Israel; for they are at hand to come.

EZEKIEL 36:10

And I will multiply men upon you, all the house of Israel, [even] all of it: and the cities shall be inhabited, and the wastes shall be builded:

Notice that phrase—he will multiply all the house of Israel on the land of Israel. Just keep that in mind; I will tell you why in just a few moments.

I love verse 11.

EZEKIEL 36:11

And I will multiply upon you man and beast; and they shall increase and bring fruit: and I will settle you after your old estates, and will do better [unto you] than at your beginnings: and ye shall know that I [am] the LORD.

He's saying, "Hey, look. Joshua and Caleb came back with a great report, said it was a land of milk and honey. I could have had the children of Israel go right in then, but the ten spies that did not come back with a positive report discouraged the people. So they didn't go in, and they wandered around for forty years."

But it was a beautiful land, the land of milk and honey. It was a forested land. It was just a marvelous piece of real estate. Not after, of course, the time of the Ottoman Empire, when it was totally devastated. All the trees were cut down and it looked almost desert-like. In fact, when Mark Twain visited the land, he said, "This is the most terrible piece of geography I've ever seen any place in the world. It's so devastated; nobody could ever sustain life here." I want you to know—and I can stand and testify, and those of you who have been there can give testimony—God has made the desert blossom like the rose, and it is coming back and it is becoming a beautiful land once again.

God said, "I will bring you into the land. And when I bring you into the land, it's going to be better than when your forefathers had the land." You want to know why He's doing this? Look at verse 22.

I knew an orthodox Jewish rabbi named Meir Kahane. You might have heard of Rabbi Kahane, as he was somewhat of a rabble-rouser. In fact, if you saw the film on ABC about 9/11, it depicted Rabbi Kahane being assassinated in 1990 by an Egyptian who was later a part of the team that took down the Twin Towers. He was speaking at a hotel in New York City. This Egyptian terrorist came in with a .357 Magnum, walked up to Rabbi Kahane, put the gun right in his face, and blew his head off.

I had witnessed to Rabbi Kahane, and I believed that Kahane was going to come to know Christ as Lord and Savior. At the time, I was the Vice President and General Manager of New York City's first Christian radio station. We had a unique programming approach, because the Jewish people who owned the radio station before Christians bought it compelled us to do orthodox Jewish programming every night for six hours. So, from 8 p.m. to 2 a.m., we did orthodox Jewish programming. Of course, the next morning when they got up, their clock radio was still tuned into what they went to sleep with, and we had Christian programming on at that time.

As Manager, in regard to every Jewish broadcaster on that station, I told my staff, "You don't talk to them. I'll do the talking to all of the Jewish broadcasters." So, they all had to come into my office. They all had to be told what, indeed, I was going to reveal to them about my salvation experience. And so, Rabbi Meir Kahane sat across from me at my desk. I didn't know what he was going to say. You see, he was one of the men who threw a bomb into the Russian embassy. He was a rabble-rousing Jew, and had founded the Jewish Defense

League. We were sitting there in my office and I looked at Rabbi Kahane and I said, "Let me tell you how I got saved." And I proceeded to tell him how I came to know Jesus Christ as my Lord and Savior at eleven years of age, as a boy in Miami, Florida, at 10:35 on a Sunday morning, in the basement of the Flagler Street Baptist Church, when Mr. Griffin, the Sunday school teacher, told me I was on my way to hell. I said, "I don't want to have to go to hell." He said, "Well, trust in Jesus." And I did, and Jesus saved me. I told the rabbi that, and I gave him the gospel and told him how to get saved. Then I looked this rabbi right square in the eye and I said, "Rabbi, if you die without Jesus Christ, you are going to burn in hell forever." Now, this is a rabble-rousing orthodox Jewish rabbi. I didn't know if he was going to bomb me, get up and shoot me, or who knows what. But I knew I had to tell him about Jesus, so I did.

I'm not always in your face, but I'll do what I need to do to have an opportunity to talk to you about Jesus Christ. I remember the very first time I started witnessing, it was to a hitchhiker. I'm not afraid of picking up a hitchhiker, and I found that it's a great way to witness. Let me tell you how I do it. I simply take my Bible, open it up, and set it in the seat beside me next to the passenger door. When I spot someone who needs a ride, I pull up and say, "Get in!" The guy comes running up to the car, and I say, "Get in, man!" He takes a look and says, "That book is in the way." "Well," I say, "move it over." He doesn't want to touch it, so he slips in between the Bible and the door. There's no way he can stab me, man, because he's too far away. Now I've got a captive audience. I remember that first guy. I pick him up, and I'm driving down the highway in South Georgia. I'm going about sixty-five miles an hour and I looked over at this dude and I said, "Hey man, are you ready to die?" "Ready to die?" he exclaims. I said, "Yeah." He said, "No, I'm not!" I asked, "Would you like to be ready?" He said, "I think so, yes."

After that, I started preaching in jails on Sunday morning. Not because I was in from Saturday night, but because I would go in on Sunday morning. This one Sunday morning I walked into a jail and I was going to give my testimony and tell these guys how to get saved, and behind the bar was this real skinny little punk. Every time I'd say something about Jesus, he'd say, "Go, Jesus! Ah ha-ha, Jesus." He was smoking cigarettes and I can't stand it when somebody blows smoke on me. I was about to die. On this particular morning I had taken this little high school guy with me. He's standing behind and, for some reason, takes his knife out and starts cleaning his fingernails. I knew I didn't have everyone's full attention, so I reached in the bars and I grabbed the punk with the cigarette and I yanked him against the bars. I reached back and I grabbed the knife from the kid behind me, and I put the knife to the guy's neck. I said, "Hey man, what would you do if I slit your throat right now?" He said, "I'd die." I said, "Where would you go if you died, man?" "I'd go to hell." I said, "Do you want me to tell you how you don't have to go to hell?" He said, "Yes, sir." I led him to Jesus Christ right there in that jail cell. You see, I first had to get his attention. Now, don't go down the street with a knife, saying, "Where you going to go, man? I'll cut your head off." But, sometimes you have to get in their face.

After I got in Rabbi Kahane's face and I told him he was going to burn in hell if he didn't know Jesus as his Lord and Savior, you know what he did? I was really amazed. He looked at me and said, "Hey, Jimmy, you know what? Because you are a fundamentalist Christian and because I'm an orthodox Jewish rabbi, that doesn't get us any credit with God; not a bit of credit." He said, "Let me tell you why God does anything for any of us." He took me to Ezekiel 36:22. Notice what it says:

EZEKIEL 36:22
Therefore say unto the house of Israel, Thus saith the Lord GOD; I do not [this] for your sakes, O house of Israel, but for mine holy name's sake, ...

When God can swear by nothing greater than His name, He said "I will disperse them because they are disobedient to me. But I will gather them and bring them back into the land. I will give them a piece of real estate like I promised their forefather Abraham." You've got some people wanting to say that God has forsaken the Jew and replaced the Jew with the church. I want to tell you, that's a lie from the pit of hell. Because, if He can lie to the Jew, He can lie to you and me about eternal salvation. But, He cannot lie, and so thus, He must keep the Abrahamic covenant. He promised to give them a nation. He must keep the land covenant. That's Deuteronomy 30. He promised to give them a piece of real estate. That's what he's saying here in chapter 36: "I will find them wherever they are; I will bring them into the land."

Borders of the Promised Land

Do you know that the Jewish people today have only ten percent of what God has promised to give them? There are thirty-eight locations in the Scriptures that talk about the Biblical borders of Israel. I won't take time now to look at them, but I'm going to give you a compilation of all of them. The borders start in the south at the river of Egypt, most likely the Nile River. Some want to debate me and call it the Wadi in Egypt, but it's exactly the same thing, the Nile River. That border then extends up the Mediterranean coast through the Sinai desert, all the way through Israel, all the way through Lebanon, continuing north to the Euphrates River. It then starts taking a southeastern turn, coming down, taking in all of Syria, all of Jordan, three-fourths of Iraq, and all of Kuwait. It gets to the Persian Gulf and goes around to the Red Sea, taking in three-fourths of Saudi Arabia, and comes back to Egypt. You want to know what the problem is in the Middle East? Hafez al-Assad emphasized it. He was the late

President and the father of the current President of Syria. He once said, "The problem in the Middle East is that these Jews believe the Bible." Hello? You're right, Hafez al-Assad.

You know what I've just told you? God has promised to give the Jews half of Egypt, all of Israel, all of Lebanon, all of Syria, all of Jordan, three-fourths of Iraq, all of Kuwait, and three-fourths of Saudi Arabia. That's what God will give the Jewish people. Not before He comes back, but during the Millennial Kingdom that lasts for one thousand years. Before the rapture and during that seven-year Tribulation period, there is going to be a continual conflict going on as these Jews just want the little ten percent of all the real estate God is going to give them. These enemies of Israel are going to attack. They are going to come in and try to take this piece of real estate. But God has promised to give them this land and He will make good on His promise. The book of Ezekiel is a prophecy of what He said He is going to do, and it's an absolute certainty that He will do it.

The Regathering

Starting in 1897, when the first Zionist Congress convened, the Jews started coming back into the land. Well, what's been going on since that time is unbelievable. Since Judy and I moved to Israel, 1.3 million Russian Jews have come to live in the land. That's an increase in the population of one nation by thirty-seven percent. That has never happened in the history of the world: in less than a decade, a thirty-seven percent increase in the population of one nation. In the book of Jeremiah, chapters 16, 23, and 31 all prophesied at the time of the end: "I will reach into the north." Russia is due north from Jerusalem, by the way. Ezekiel 5:5 says Jerusalem is the center of the earth; all the nations are around her. So, all direction in the Bible is based on Jerusalem and due north is the nation of Russia. In all, 1.3 million have come to be in the land.

May 24, 1991 was a Friday afternoon. Now, on Friday afternoon at sundown the Sabbath begins. The trains don't move, the planes don't fly, automobiles are parked, and the buses don't run. It's the Sabbath and for 24 hours they honor God by not doing all the things that they would normally do. But, on that afternoon, forty-two aircraft took off from Ben Gurion International Airport; they flew across southern Israel, across the Red Sea, and into Addis Ababa, Ethiopia. Meanwhile, in Addis Ababa, fifteen thousand Ethiopian Jews were making their way over to the airport. In the next 24 hours, all fifteen thousand Ethiopian Jews would be transported to Israel in the greatest airlift to take place in the history of the world. There were twenty-eight aircraft in the air at one time. One jumbo jet normally carried about five hundred people. However, for this flight, every seat was taken out; they got one thousand eighty-seven people on that one airplane. While it was flying into Jerusalem, seven babies were born on the plane. They landed at Ben Gurion International Airport, and then came over to Jerusalem. Mr. and Mrs. Journalist (Jimmy and Judy) go down to meet them. I'm going to cover this story. I had my microphone, and I'm going to go down there and do some interviewing. I get down there and discover that they don't speak Hebrew, they don't speak English, and I don't speak their language. I'm kind of useless. Judy's the photographer in our crew and she was taking her pictures. As the famished travelers were heading downstairs for a meal, I motioned to Judy, "Hey, honey, we need to go help them eat." I walked downstairs and all these Ethiopian Jews who had been starving to death were seated at the table. The Israelis had placed before each of them a plate that had a boiled egg on it, a container of yogurt, and some olives, pickles, tomatoes, cucumbers, and onions. Just normal fare; what we eat in Israel. But the Ethiopians didn't know how to eat it. They had never seen a boiled egg. Where they came from, they ate the chicken, if it was around; they didn't wait for it to drop an egg. They were starving, but didn't know what a boiled egg was. So I took this boiled egg, cracked it, peeled it, and showed this old man how to eat it. He started eating his. Then I looked and saw a lady who had a baby strapped to her back. I walked over, opened up the yogurt container, took the spoon, and started feeding the baby. When I began feeding her, it started to catch on. As I was doing that, the tears were streaming down my face, because I remembered Zephaniah 3:10

says, "At the time of the end, I will reach into Ethiopia, I will get my prize and I will bring them into Jerusalem." And I was privileged to actually be touching the fulfillment of that prophecy.

The Hebrew Language

By the way, when you say the word "Aliyah," you have touched the fulfillment of prophecy. That word means to go up to Jerusalem. It's Hebrew. You know what? A dead language, Hebrew, was restored. In God's Word, Zephaniah 3:9, says, "When I bring the people into the land, I will restore their language." You just touched fulfilled prophecy with your lips by saying "Aliyah." He's brought them back into the land. They speak Hebrew, which we are going to be speaking forever in heaven, so you'd better start learning it. God is doing some unbelievable things.

Go back to Ezekiel 37, and let me show you something. You may have heard or read in the news some of the things I've just talked about—the return of the Jews back to the land. This miraculous incident has been taking place annually; there are many Jews from many nations making their way back into the land. I can give countless examples, such as in 2010 three thousand Jews from North America made their way back into the land. And these people, when they get there, they kiss the airport tarmac they are so excited and say, "We're home! We're home!"

Twelve Tribes in the Land

Remember when the war was going on between Israel and Hezbollah in southern Lebanon? The Jews were coming in by large numbers. The prime minister went out to meet them and said, "You are the greatest strength we have, you Jews coming home in our time of need." That's what is going on. The regathering is in the process of being fulfilled. You cannot deny what God is doing with the Jewish people. But there's one other thing I want to show you:

> EZEKIEL 37:15-17
>
> *The word of the LORD came again unto me, saying,*
>
> *Moreover, thou son of man, take thee one stick, and write upon it, For Judah, and for the children of Israel his companions: then take another stick, and write upon it, For Joseph, the stick of Ephraim, and [for] all the house of Israel his companions:*
>
> *And join them one to another into one stick; and they shall become one in thine hand.*

Now if you read that, it's almost like double talk. Let me show you exactly what this passage of Scripture says. God tells Ezekiel to take two sticks. On one stick, put Judah; on the other stick, put Israel. When he has these two sticks, one in each hand, he is to put the two sticks into one hand and while the two sticks are in his one hand, those two sticks will become one stick. That's a prophecy. He's talking about what's going to take place. He's talking about a time after the Jews come into the land. Let me just give you this hint. Chapter 38 is the alignment of the nations, when they form a coalition to come against the Jewish state and those nations that are listed there are the Islamic nations of the world. So between the time when the Jews started coming into the land and when the nations go against Israel, he says, "take two sticks, Judah and Israel, put them in your hand, the two become one."

Now, maybe you've thought about that a little bit, and maybe you think, well, I know what that's talking about. In chapter 11 of First Kings, after King Solomon had reigned for forty years as king, one of his adversaries, Jeroboam, decided to divide the twelve tribes. So Jeroboam, who was from Beth-El, a part of the tribe of Ephraim, took ten of the tribes and they went to the north to a place called Dan to live. The other two tribes, Benjamin and Judah, stayed in the south and Rehoboam, who was Solomon's son, became king of Judah. So the Jewish people were divided. Maybe you've heard some television program on one of those weird cable networks that talks about the ten lost tribes of Israel. "We found them! We know where they are! They are gathering in now." That is not what this is talking about. There is no such thing as ten lost tribes of Israel. Get it out of your mind. No Jew is lost as it relates to not being found by his own people. They are all lost and on their way to hell, though, if they don't know Jesus Christ as Lord and Savior. But there is no such thing as ten lost tribes.

There are no "Lost Tribes" of Israel

Let me prove my point. Go to the book of Ezra. I want you to notice what happens in the book of Ezra. The first chapter in Ezra is a record of fulfilled prophecy. Over in Isaiah 44:28, God told the prophet Isaiah to prophesy about a man who would be raised up after the Babylonian captivity, a man who would give the Jewish people the right to return to Jerusalem and rebuild the Temple. In fact, in Isaiah's prophecy, it even names the man: his name would be Cyrus. Now, here's one of the ways you authenticate the Word of God. Isaiah's prophecy, one hundred fifty years before the fact, was about a man named Cyrus, who would allow the Jews to go back and rebuild their Temple. Then Ezra, one hundred fifty years after Isaiah made the prophecy, records what happened, and it's exactly as Isaiah prophesied.

> EZRA 1:2-3
> *Thus saith Cyrus king of Persia, The LORD God of heaven hath given me all the kingdoms of the earth; and he hath charged me to build him an house at Jerusalem, which [is] in Judah.*
>
> *Who [is there] among you of all of his people? his God be with him, and let him go up to Jerusalem, which [is] in Judah, and build the house of the LORD God of Israel, (he [is] the God,) which [is] in Jerusalem.*

So it is that that prophecy was fulfilled. Chapter 1 tells us it was Zerubbabel who he chose. Chapter 2 is a record of those people going back. There were 49,897 people (almost fifty thousand people) who go back to Jerusalem to build the Temple. Now there are seventy verses here, and I'm not going to take the time to go to all seventy verses. I will just point out two of them for you to see what I'm trying to prove.

> EZRA 2:28
>
> *The men of Beth-el and Ai, two hundred twenty and three.*

In other words, he's documenting how many people are going to go back to Beth-El. Now, if you were paying attention just a moment ago, I told you that Jeroboam, the one who rebelled against King Solomon, took ten of the twelve tribes, took them to the north and they became known as Israel. He was from Beth-El, which is the tribe of Ephraim. It's not the two southern tribes, Benjamin and Judah, it's Ephraim. He takes them to the north, but his people come back into the land.

Let me show you one more.

> EZRA 2:29
>
> *The children of Nebo, fifty and two.*

Nebo is on the eastern side of the Jordan River, in the mountains of Moab. Nebo is where Moses went, looked into the Promised Land, but was not allowed to go in. However, at that point in time, he was told that

Joshua was going to lead the children of Israel into the Promised Land. By the way, who got the tribe of Nebo, what tribe stayed there? Well, half of the tribe of Manasseh went up to the Golan Heights, Gad got Gilead, and Reuben got Moab. So we are talking about another of the tribes of Israel, not the two.

In the sixth chapter of Ezra, we see the dedicatory service take place for the Temple that is going to be built. This is a record. In chapters 5 and 6, we see the Temple is completed under the preaching of Zechariah and Haggai. In Ezra 5:1, it tells about the two prophets who preach. They finish building the Temple in chapter 6.

EZRA 6:15

And this house was finished on the third day of the month Adar, which was in the sixth year of the reign of Darius the king.

The word "Israel" is used in one of three ways in the Bible. First, it is used as the name of Jacob (Genesis 32), when God changed Jacob's name to Israel. Second, it is used to describe all twelve tribes. And third, it is used to describe the ten tribes that went to the north. It is never used to describe the two tribes—Benjamin and Judah—that stayed in the south. So he is talking about all of Israel. That is what he says—the children of Israel, the priests, and the Levites. By the way, the priests and the Levites come from the tribe of Levi, not those two other southern tribes, Benjamin and Judah. So there's a third tribe it is talking about.

EZRA 6:16-17

And the children of Israel, the priests, and the Levites, and the rest of the children of the captivity, kept the dedication of this house of God with joy,

And offered at the dedication of this house of God an hundred bullocks, two hundred rams, four hundred lambs; ....

That's a pretty good offering taking place. Now notice this:

EZRA 6:17 (continued)

... and for a sin offering for all Israel, ...

All of Israel, who is back in the land.

EZRA 6:17 (continued)

... twelve he goats, according to the number of the tribes of Israel.

All twelve tribes are in the land. The book of Ezra was written twenty-five hundred years ago. Twenty-five hundred years ago, all twelve tribes were back in the land. All of Israel was there.

Go to Matthew 10. This is the record of Jesus Christ sending his disciples out two by two. He gathers them in to instruct them. Notice what He tells them:

MATTHEW 10:5-6

These twelve Jesus sent forth, and commanded them saying, Go not into the way of the Gentiles, and into [any] city of the Samaritans enter ye not:

But go rather to the lost sheep of the house of Israel.

So two thousand years ago, all twelve tribes were in the land. If you go to Acts 2:5, it says there were Jews from every nation of the world gathered in Jerusalem on the day of Pentecost after Christ had left, some fifty days after His resurrection and that period of time He had spent on the earth after the resurrection.

So it is that all twelve tribes were in the land. Now having said that, go back to Ezekiel 37. What is this prophecy talking about? What is it dealing with here when it says all twelve tribes? Let me just give you another bit of information. The book of Ezekiel uses the words "Judah" and "Israel." It uses the word "Judah" eighteen times. It uses the word "Israel" one hundred sixty-nine times. It's talking to Israel, all twelve tribes. All twelve tribes are in the land. All twelve tribes, since the time of Ezra, have been in the land. Since the time of Jesus Christ, all twelve tribes were in the land; on the day of Pentecost all twelve tribes were in the land.

Two Jewish Nations

Before the rapture of the church, all twelve tribes will be in the land. When the rapture of the church takes place, all twelve tribes will be in the land. Then, they will become two different Jewish states—Israel and Judah. When do they come back together? Let's see what the Lord says to Ezekiel. They were going to ask him what happened when these sticks were in his hand, and here's what God said to tell them:

> EZEKIEL 37:21
>
> *... Thus saith the Lord GOD; Behold, I will take the children of Israel from among the heathen, whither they be gone, and will gather them on every side, and bring them into their own land.*

That's what I've been talking about—the valley of dry bones: the bones coming together, the flesh coming on the bones; the regathering of the Jewish people, the restoration of a Jewish state. All of this is taking place even as we have been watching in the last several years. "I'm going to bring them into the land." Now that's settled, God's going to bring them into the land as all twelve tribes.

> EZEKIEL 37:22
>
> *And I will make them one nation in the land upon the mountains of Israel; ...*

They will become one nation again in the land. Now the truth is, they go into the land as one nation, they become two, and then they will be made one again. When does that happen? It happens at the end of the Tribulation, that seven-year period of time.

110

EZEKIEL 37:23

Neither shall they defile themselves anymore with their idols, nor with their detestable things, nor with any of their transgressions: but I will save them out of all their dwellingplaces, wherein they have sinned, and will cleanse them: so shall they be my people, and I will be their God.

When does this happen? When will the Jewish people again become the children of God and God again become their God? When Jesus Christ comes back.

Zechariah 3:9 prophesies that the Jewish people turn to Jesus Christ in one day. So what happens is, all twelve tribes become one nation—Israel. Now here's what's coming: The rapture of the church; one nation (Israel) becomes two nations (Israel and Judah), and they continue that way through the seven-year period of Tribulation; the revelation, when Jesus Christ comes back; two nations become one again. Is that possible? Not only is it possible, it's absolutely going to happen.

Ehud Olmert, former Prime Minister of Israel, said, "We will evacuate Judea and Samaria (the West Bank), because the European Union, the United States, the United Nations, and Russia say it's not right to have that land. It must be given to the Palestinians."

Five hundred thousand Jews live in Judea and Samaria. That's ten percent of the population of the state of Israel. Those five hundred thousand Jews went into that land at the behest of Ariel Sharon, after the Six-

Day War in 1967, to become a buffer zone between Israel and Jordan, Israel and Syria, and Israel and Egypt. They've lived there, they've built their homes, they've raised their families, and they've started their businesses.

Part of that area is the Temple Mount in Jerusalem, the most sacred piece of real estate for any Jew. It is the center of the earth. It's where Jesus has chosen to dwell among His people forever and ever. It is the original site and the future site of the Garden of Eden.

The Israeli government is ready to give that land away. In the summer of 2005, they extracted the Jews, some ten thousand of them out of twenty-five Jewish settlements in the Gaza Strip. What happened? Hamas came in and started killing Jews. These Jews in Judea and Samaria say they are not coming out.

Ehud Olmert said, "We're going to evacuate them."

Ten thousand Jews went into Homash, which was a Jewish settlement in the north, and the Israeli Defense Force went in there and ripped them out of that location. I called and asked some of them, "What are you going to do?"

The spokesman said, "If the Israeli government comes in to put us out of here, we're not going to go."

I said, "Well, they'll come in with force, with the Israeli Defense Force."

He said, "If they come in with military might, we will take up our weapons and kill anybody who tries to take us out."

Then I asked, "Well, is that the best thing to do?"

He said, "No it's not. But that may be the only thing we can do. We are not leaving the land that God has given us. This is God-given land. He promised to give it to us, and we are here because of what He's done; we can't leave it."

So I asked, "Is there another alternative?"

He said, "To establish a second Jewish state."

The man leading that movement was quoted in the Jerusalem Post as saying that the only solution to where Israel is today is a second Jewish state.

During the last trip Ariel Sharon made to the Texas White House, he stood in front of President George W. Bush and he made the following statement. "Mr. President, my nation is on the verge of civil war. Not Israel against Arabs, but Israel against Israel, Jew against Jew. We could go to civil war at any point."

That was the former Prime Minister's statement. Now Ehud Olmert, the man who followed him as Prime Minister, said, "We will pull them out."

They said, "We will take up our weapons." But one man with some type of thinking ability, a leading lawyer in the city of Jerusalem named Ben-Joseph, said the only alternative is a second Jewish state.

I called Mr. Ben-Joseph and I asked, "Sir, how close is this Jewish state?"

He said, "Well, go see one of my partners in this venture, Yoel Learner, in the old city."

I walked into the old city, right down the street from where they are preparing to build the next Temple, and I saw Yoel Learner. I asked, "Sir, how close are you to a second Jewish state?"

He gave me a Constitution for the state of Judah. It's all set. They are ready to have a second Jewish state.

Ezekiel, twenty-five hundred years ago, said when they come into the land, they will form a second Jewish state—Israel and Judah. But before they form that state, that second Jewish state, we Christians are out of here. We go to be with Jesus. Folks, there is one Jewish state, the rapture happens, two Jewish states are formed, then Jesus Christ comes back. Never in the history of the world has it been just like this. Never. We are watching it.

Israel and Judah are ready to be formed. Every single day, fulfillment of this prophecy gets closer and closer and closer. All that has to happen is the rapture (which could occur at any time), then the events we've been studying will begin to unfold. That's how close we are. If we are that close—the state of Judah, the state of Israel, the coming of the Lord—how close are we? We are going to meet Him. And if that close, how then ought we to live?

Islam and the Alignment of Nations

In our outline of the book of Ezekiel, chapters 25 through 32 are a message of retribution to the neighbors, or the enemies, of the Jewish people. I'm not going to go to that particular passage, but there is that information there available for you.

In addition to that, the prophet to the nations was Jeremiah. The last twenty chapters of Jeremiah deal with the nations as well. Individual books in the Bible deal with particular nations that are involved in the end-times scenario that is laid out in God's Word. We read much about the nations, what they are doing in that part of the world and we need to have a better understanding of what is going on. We are also going to look at the Islamic world; where they came from, who the father of Islam was. I'm talking about the original father of Islam, not Mohammed, who happens to be the prophet of Islam. We will see how the Islamic world plays into end-time prophecy; what is going to happen to the Islamic people, and the militant Islamic people, as well.

Six thousand years ago is when Jesus Christ created the heavens, the earth, and all that in them is. Four thousand years after that, Jesus Christ was born on this earth, lived, died, was buried, resurrected, then went to heaven. Now today, two thousand years later, we are approaching the next main event in God's calendar of activities—the rapture of the church. After that, there is going to be a seven-year period of time, the seven years of Tribulation; seven years of terrible trouble upon the face of the earth. This will be a time referred to by Jeremiah 30:7 as "the time of Jacob's trouble." It will be a terrible time of judgment. There are reasons for this Tribulation. One of those reasons is to evangelize the Jew.

There will be two witnesses who will preach during the first three-and-one-half years of the seven years. Those two witnesses will, in their first activities, lead one hundred forty-four thousand male virgin Jews to Jesus Christ. Those male virgin Jews talked about in Revelation 14 will spread across the world and, during this seven-year period of time on earth, every single person is going to have an opportunity to hear the gospel of the kingdom and have an opportunity to receive or reject Jesus Christ. That's talked about in Matthew 24:14. That verse is not talking about today. Now, I love missionaries (I am one), but don't let a missionary say, "We've got to get the gospel out to the entire world before Jesus Christ comes back, so send me out to these peoples I am going to." That is not correct.

One of the purposes, during this seven-year Tribulation, is to reach the entire world with the gospel. Everybody will hear the gospel of the kingdom; every single person. These one hundred forty-four thousand Jewish evangelists will spread across the world during this seven-year period of time. At the end of the seven years, Jesus Christ will come back to the earth and there is then going to be a one-thousand-year period of time—the Millennial Kingdom. Chapters 40 through 46 in Ezekiel deal with that period of time. After that, the Great White Throne Judgment; a time of retribution, when Jesus will be the judge, sentencing those who have rejected Him to the lake of fire, which is the second death. Then eternity future, with a new heaven, a new earth, and a new Jerusalem.

God's Promise of the Land

In Ezekiel 38, we now start to see the Jewish people returning to the land. Remember that chapter 37 was the bones coming together and the flesh coming on the bones, representing the Jewish people being gathered from around the world and the restoration of a Jewish state—the only time in the history of the world when a people come out from the known world and form again the state that they once had. They will come and they will establish this state. In fact, there will be two Jewish states before the return of Jesus Christ.

God has promised to give the Jewish people ten times the amount of real estate that they have today. He's promised to give them half of Egypt, all of Israel, all of Lebanon, all of Syria, all of Jordan, three-fourths of Iraq, all of Kuwait, and three-fourths of Saudi Arabia. That's the land mass that God is going to give the Jewish people and that is a forever possession they will have. The word "forever" in Hebrew is "olam." That's the same word with the name of God, El-Olam. Of course, the names of God talk about the character of God. El-Olam is talking about the longevity of God. He is forever, He had no beginning, He has no ending. When you take the word "olam" away from El-Olam and put it with another bit of information, it's talking about the exact same thing. We are not going to see this land given to the Jewish people until the end of the thousand-year Millennial Kingdom. That land is going to be given to them forever; on the new earth they are going to have that piece of real estate. In fact, the Jewish people will have the land on the earth and that's where they will be headquartered during eternity future. We will have a different location. We'll be in the new Jerusalem, which will not be on the earth.

God has promised this land to the Jewish people. They are coming into the land right now, and Ezekiel 37 says they come into the land in unbelief. Remember what I said? They are regathered in unbelief, they are restored in unbelief. That's exactly where they are today. Israel is not a religious state. Twenty-nine percent of the population of Israel may be religious. Not Christian, of course, but they are religious, involved in what is termed as rabbinical Judaism. Rabbinical Judaism is basically Satanic, because they denounce Jesus Christ, they say He was not the Son of God. When you look at I John 4, we are told that anybody who says that Jesus Christ was not the Son of God in the living flesh is an antichrist.

Alignment of Nations

One of the major trends in our world today, that you can look at and recognize as an unfolding event that gives indication, or evidence, that we are very close to the revelation (second coming) of Christ, is the alignment of the nations against Israel.

And just consider this: if we are close to the second coming and the rapture takes place before the second coming, would it not be smart to think, well, if that's about to happen, and this must happen seven years earlier, then maybe it's about to happen pretty soon? It's just logical thinking. So, when I talk about these events that unfold after the rapture, they should give us the urgency of the moment for the rapture.

Let me just show you one verse in Ezekiel that is essential for our understanding of why Jerusalem is going to be the focus of this world.

> EZEKIEL 5:5
> *Thus saith the Lord GOD; This [is] Jerusalem: I have set it in the midst of the nations and countries [that are] round about her.*

God placed Jerusalem in the center of the earth. (I love it in Hebrew, it sounds so beautiful: Yerushalayim.) He had a purpose. He brings the Jew into existence. He gives them this nation for the purpose of being those witnesses who will give testimony of the reality of a pure, perfect, almighty, Holy God. Even the secular Jew today is walking evidence of a God who is almighty, who is powerful, who can do what He said He was going to do, because He has sustained them for four thousand years. That's amazing! No other people can claim that. So even a secular Jew, who has no idea of religion at all, is a testimony; a walking, living testimony of what God is going to do. So, He puts Jerusalem in the center of the earth with all the countries around her. They are to give testimony of the blessing received when you are obedient. Of course they receive the Word of God. In Romans 3, they will preserve the Word of God and they will communicate, or transmit, the Word of God to the world. So God had a reason for placing Jerusalem in the center of the earth and giving that land to the Jewish people.

But because of that, the enemies of the Jewish people are not going to stand still. Who is the motivator behind these enemies of the Jewish people? Satan. When he realized there was a Messiah coming, in Genesis 3:15, what did he do? He contaminated the human race. If from the loins of a beautiful Jewish girl one day would come forth the Messiah, he had to shut that out. Remember, in Job 38 we learned that the sons of God were angels. In Genesis 6, we see that these sons of God had sexual relationships with the daughters of men. Satan found a way to contaminate the human race. The flood, then, was God's response to this contamination.

Did you ever wonder why there is a genealogy in Genesis 5, just before the record of the flood in chapters 6, 7, and 8? You can learn something from genealogies. That genealogy in Genesis 5 starts with Adam and it concludes with Noah. You know what? There is not one evil angel listed in that genealogy. That's why in chapter 6, God said, "I find Noah perfect." Not perfect without sin; all of us have been born in sin. "Perfect" in that he doesn't have any evil angelic strain in his bloodline. There is not one listed there. He is pure. He is that individual that will then leap over that flood period, when all of humankind—except for eight souls—will be destroyed. Those eight souls, then, have responsibility for starting the next "batch" of humankind.

Satan will now try to destroy the Jewish people when they come into the land in the last days. I'm going to show you the people he has selected to try to wipe out the Jewish people and the reasons behind it. As we look at the Palestinian people for the end times, they are part of Satan's plan. Why do you think there was a Holocaust? Why do you think there was a Spanish Inquisition? Why do you think there has been anti-Semitism rampant across the world? Because if Satan can wipe out the Jew, what happens? God's plan fails and God is no longer God. If He can't keep His promise, He's not God. If He lies, He's not God. So, why do you think the church has gone into a mode of anti-Semitism when they claim to have replaced the Jew? Any church that says, "We have replaced the Jew, there is no program for Israel in the future," is satanic. I say this because they are endeavoring to try to rid the world of Jews through religion.

You know why the Holocaust occurred? It came about because of Martin Luther, the father of the Reformation. Martin Luther saw that grace was the way, not works, and he changed, but he kept some of his baggage with him. His eschatology was wrong. Martin Luther wrote books, preached sermons, and wrote songs that were anti-Semitic: destroy the Jew, they have turned against God, we must replace them. That was a replacement theology coming from his background and he never got rid of that. Who established the mother church of Germany, the Lutheran church? Martin Luther. I'm not saying Martin Luther wasn't a born-again believer, I'm simply saying he had a wrong theology that became slightly off with the passing of time; and after four hundred years it became a chasm that enabled the Holocaust. I'm not saying the Lutheran people were responsible for the Holocaust. I'm saying they are responsible for not stopping the Holocaust. They stood by and Hitler went in and killed the Jews. They were just standing there, because of a wrong theology. Understand what I'm saying? That's exactly what God is going to watch over, as Satan moves to try to destroy the Jewish people. Now, He is going to intercede. He's going to save the Jews. He's not going to let them all be destroyed, but there is going to be a lead-up to this.

That's what we come to in Ezekiel 38.

EZEKIEL 38:1-2

And the word of the LORD came unto me, saying,

Son of man, set thy face against Gog, the land of Magog, ...

Now, Gog is the personality, and Magog is the land. The chief prince of Meshech and Tubal prophesy against him. Then he continues on, in verse 5, with the nations that are going to be involved against Israel: Persia, Ethiopia, and Libya. In verse 6:

EZEKIEL 38:6

Gomer, and all his bands; the house of Togarmah of the north quarters, and all his bands: [and] many people with thee."

So we read here, in Ezekiel 38, the beginnings of the alignment of nations; a coalition of nations that are going to come against Israel.

Now let me tell you that, as you approach your study of nations, you must remember there is a hermeneutical principle as it relates to Biblical geography. Hermeneutics is the science of interpreting Scripture. Hermeneutical principles are used in every aspect of interpretation of Scripture and, in particular, in Biblical geography. The hermeneutical principle is, "Who was the author writing about when he wrote the book?" In other words, when Ezekiel wrote this book twenty-five hundred years ago, who was he thinking about? Who was on his mind when he mentioned Magog, Meshech, Tubal, Gomer, Togarmah, Persia, Ethiopia, and Libya? Who was he talking about? That's a good question. I would suggest the answer can be found in a two-volume commentary published by the Dallas Theological Seminary: *The Bible Knowledge Commentary*. It's a conservative commentary, but deals with the issues. In that commentary, they list the nations that are talked about in the Scriptures in Biblical times. And they put them on a map. Let me tell you what they have conveyed to us in their research.

During the time of Ezekiel, Magog was a piece of real estate that was north of the Caspian and Black Seas. He referred to it as Magog then, but today we know it as Russia. Meshech, Tubal, Gomer, and Togarmah, were the four sections that Turkey was divided into during Biblical times. So when you come to this, we are talking about Turkey. We are not talking about Germany because Gomer sounds like Germany. No, we are talking about Turkey. Who was Ezekiel writing about? He had no idea of Germany twenty-five hundred years ago. He was writing down what he knew to be locations. Then in verse 5, it talks about Persia, Ethiopia, and Libya. Maybe your translation says Cush instead of Ethiopia, or maybe your translation says Put instead of Libya. Some of the countries are names we recognize today, but the boundaries may have been different in Ezekiel's time. Persia included the three nations we know today as

Afghanistan, Pakistan, and Iran. Ethiopia (or Cush) is Ethiopia, Somalia, and Sudan. Libya (or Put) is Libya. These are the nations that are listed here.

Go to Daniel 11 just a moment. It gives us two other nations who will be a part of this coalition that is going to come against the Jewish people in the end times. Starting in verse 36 it is referring to Antichrist. Then in verses 40 and 41, it refers to the king of the south and the king of the north. Early on in chapter 11, the king of the south rules over what we know today as modern-day Egypt. The king of the north is modern-day Syria. So what we are talking about here in this passage of Scripture is that modern-day Egypt (in the south), and modern-day Syria (in the north), will attack him. It says in verse 40, attack "him," the Antichrist.

Time between the Rapture and the Tribulation

After the rapture of the church, I talked about a seven-year period of time. Let me just clarify a little bit, because that is not quite correct. (Now, this is man's illustration, so it can fall to some extent.) After the rapture of the church, there is going to be a period of time before the seven years of Tribulation begins. How long a period? I do not know. The Bible is totally silent on it. It's likely going to be a short period of time.

What has to happen during that time, before the seven-year Tribulation starts? First, the ten horns of Daniel 7 have to come into existence. That would be the revived Roman Empire. Then out of that, the little horn must come. ("Little horn" is one of twenty-seven names for the Antichrist.) And finally, as prophesied in Daniel 9:27, the Antichrist will confirm a peace agreement with Israel. So those three things have to happen after the rapture of the church and before the seven years. You see, the clock starts ticking on the seven years when that peace treaty is confirmed.

DANIEL 9:27

And he shall confirm the covenant with many for one week: ....

How long will it take? Nobody knows and that's not talked about in the Bible. My guess is that it will be a very short period of time, because we have the European Union in place to become the revived Roman Empire, and the Antichrist I believe is alive and well on planet Earth, ready to be energized by Satan, and indeed everybody is talking about peace. Peace talks, or at least preparations for peace talks, are going on in the city of Jerusalem. So, before the Tribulation begins, these things will take place.

Now when the Antichrist confirms a peace treaty, he is, in the minds of all of those who deal with him, equivalent with Israel, because he's promised them he's going to take care of them. They think he's the Messiah. So when he is attacked, it's like an attack on Israel; or when Israel is attacked, it's like an attack on the Antichrist. Verse 41 says that he will rush back in. Where will he be? He will be in the seven-hilled city of

Rome, Italy. He will rush back into the Middle East to come to the defense of Israel because he's confirmed a peace treaty with them.

DANIEL 11:41

He shall enter also into the glorious land, and many [countries] shall be overthrown: ....

He goes up north and wipes out Syria. But notice that when he heads down to the south, he does not touch Edom, Moab, and Ammon. Well, that is the Biblical terminology for modern-day Jordan. Why doesn't he touch Jordan? Because of a place called Petra, which is the impregnable city that is going to house the Jewish people for the last three-and-one-half years of the Tribulation, protecting them from any harm. It is talked about in Revelation 12:6, "*a place prepared of God*" for their protection. The Antichrist doesn't touch them.

He goes to the south (Daniel 11:42), and he destroys Egypt. Then, when he destroys Egypt, he turns around. Look at verse 43. All of a sudden, the Libyans and the Ethiopians shall be at his steps, and there will be tidings out of the east and out of the north. Now that would be Iran, Afghanistan, and Pakistan (east) and Russia (north). So the nations listed in Ezekiel 38 are referred to in Daniel 11 as those nations. But what it tells us is, the first two nations to come against the Jewish state will be Syria from the north and Egypt from the south.

World Briefing

Is that a possibility? There are ten thousand Syrian soldiers at the northeastern border of Israel. They are under military exercise. They are being trained by agents from Hezbollah in guerilla-type warfare. Recently, the foreign minister of Syria said, "the next war with Israel will be ballistic." They have just made a deal with Iran to put all of those rockets on alert, ready to attack any place in Israel. Syria has the class-C SCUD rocket, the most sophisticated of the SCUD rockets. They also have biological warheads, they have biological chemical factories, and they can make biological and chemical warheads that can be mounted on those SCUD-C's and hit any location in Israel. That's right now. Syria has made the statement, "If Israel does not come to the peace table and give us back the Golan Heights diplomatically, we will take it militarily." The Israeli Defense Force is on high alert that Syria may come at any time to attack Israel. Twenty five hundred years ago, Daniel and Ezekiel laid it out, naming who was going to come. Recently, Egypt held military exercises in the Sinai desert. When asked by a journalist, the minister of defense said, "The reason we are holding these exercises is we are getting ready for war." The journalist said, "For war with whom? Who is your enemy?" The minister of defense said, "The Zionist state. We are getting ready to go after the Zionist state." The Zionist state, of course, is Israel.

Then we come to the other nations talked about in the Scriptures. Go back to Ezekiel 38, for prophecy about Russia. Russians have been the ones responsible for giving to Iran all of the technology and the technicians to develop a nuclear weapon of mass destruction. Israel has sent delegation after delegation to Russia with this request: "Please don't give any more nuclear technology or send any more nuclear technicians into Iran. They are developing a weapon of mass destruction." Israeli intelligence says Iran's weapon of mass destruction could be ready at any time (and it appears that will be sooner rather than later). They have Shahab missiles—long-range, mid-range, and short-range—that can deliver a nuclear warhead to any location in the state of Israel. By the way, America better be ready, because that long-range Shahab missile can be launched high enough in the sky for a nuclear weapon to be blown up that could shut down the entire electrical grid in this nation. They are developing a nuclear weapon of mass destruction. There is no question about it, and it's not up for debate. That's exactly what they are doing. Ahmadinejad, president of Iran, believes we are living in the apocalyptic age. He believes that he will bring the twelfth Imam, the Islamic Mahdi, or messiah. Islam has an eschatology. They believe a messiah is coming, and that he's headed toward Jerusalem to head up his headquarters in the city of Jerusalem for the one-world empire that Islam is going to put in place.

By the way, I don't know if you've noticed the demographics on Russia lately. By the year 2012, Russia will be fifty percent Islamic. Islam is growing faster in Russia than any other nation of the world. The Russian Orthodox Church is being put in second place. In 2010, fifty percent of Russia's military was Islamic. We'd better pay attention to those demographics. These aren't my demographics; that's coming out of the Russian government's own report for its own nation. That is developing quickly.

Do you know what happened in Turkey? Tayyip Erdogan was the mayor of Istanbul. He was taken out of his position as mayor by the Turkish military. The Turkish military believes they are the custodians for a secular Islamic state. I don't understand that. It sounds like an oxymoron to me. How can you be Islamic and secular at the same time? I don't know. But anyway, that's what they think they are doing. Turkey is ninety-nine percent Islamic in their faith. Tayyip Erdogan is a radical Islamic. When he was taken out as mayor of Istanbul, he established a new political party. They ran for the Parliamentary election, were elected as the majority, and formed the last government. They then changed the constitution of the nation to allow Tayyip Erdogan to run and become appointed as Prime Minister. He was appointed by his party as Prime Minister. In a recent election, his Islamic fundamentalist political party won. They are the most powerful political operation now in Turkey, and he is an Islamic. He wants to institute an Islamic republic, which would be living under the Sharia law. He is now in position. The military is at the point of bringing down the Turkish government and they may bring it down because of this recent election. They've done it already three times; they may do it a fourth time.

Do I need to say anything about Afghanistan and Pakistan? Pakistan is the only Islamic nation, as of today, that has the nuclear weapon, a weapon of mass destruction which could be potentially used by Middle Eastern Islamic terrorists. In fact, America's most-wanted terrorist, Osama bin Laden (killed by U.S. Navy SEALs in 2011), was found hiding in Pakistan. Other countries harboring terrorists include Ethiopia, Somalia, and Sudan. At one time, Sudan was headquarters for Osama Bin Laden. The Muslims are killing the Christians, two million of them killed. In Sudan there have been confirmed killings of Christians by Islamic terrorists. All of these countries are listed in the Scriptures.

I don't look at the current events first and then try to make my understanding of Bible prophecy based on what's happening today. That's backward. I look first at what the Bible says prophetically about a nation, a people, a region, and then look at current events in light of Bible prophecy. Political situations, military situations, economic situations—they all change, but God's Word never changes.

God's Judgment on the Nations

In Psalm 83, the psalmist is praying to God. Notice what he says in his prayer.

PSALM 83:1-3

Keep not thou silence, O God: hold not thy peace, and be not still, O God.

For, lo, thine enemies make a tumult: and they that hate thee have lifted up the head.

They have taken crafty counsel against thy people, and consulted against thy hidden ones.

Now notice what they are going to say when they have this conference and come together.

PSALM 83:4

They have said, Come, and let us cut them off from [being] a nation; that the name of Israel may be no more in remembrance.

We want to wipe them out; forget their name forever.

Let me just show you the names of a couple of countries that we haven't already mentioned. Look at verse 6, the *"tabernacles of Edom."* That's the Palestinians and I'll talk about them more in depth. Look at the next one, the Ishmaelites. That's modern-day Saudi Arabia, and I'll explain that in just a moment. Look at the last one, in verse 6, the Hagarenes. That would be modern-day Iran. That is a country to the east of Jerusalem. Then in verse 7, the last one listed in that verse is Tyre. Tyre and Sidon, that's modern-day Lebanon. In verse 8, Assur is modern-day Syria.

It was July 9, 2006, in Tehran, and four thousand Islamic Arab leaders had gathered together. Ahmadinejad, president of Iran, was addressing the crowd. Here's what he said, "We must rise up as Moslems and wipe Israel off the face of the earth, that their name may be forgotten forever." That's almost verbatim from his text, "that their name may be forgotten forever." That was July 9, 2006. On July 12, Hezbollah broke across the northern border of Israel, killed some Israeli Defense Force soldiers, took two of them captive, and then ensued a thirty-four day war where the invincible Israeli Defense Force was brought down, according to their perception. It was all under the context, "we must wipe Israel off the face of the earth, that their name may be forgotten forever."

"Arab" versus "Islamic" and Ishmael

You might be thinking, "All those nations are Arab nations." Actually, they are not all Arab—but they are all Islamic. There is a difference between Arab and Islamic.

Ishmael did not start the Arab world. Go back to Genesis 16 and let me show you something. It talks about the birth of Ishmael. Let me prove—in one statement, one sentence, one verse—that Ishmael did not father the Arab world.

GENESIS 16:1

> *Now Sarai Abram's wife bare him no children: and she had an handmaid, an Egyptian, whose name [was] Hagar.*

Now I have a Ph.D., not an M.D., so I might be wrong, but I think it is impossible for a son to father his mother. Do you want me to take my tongue out of my cheek now? Ishmael did not father the Egyptians. His mother was one of them.

Genesis 10 is a genealogy of the sons of Noah: Shem, Ham, and Japheth. Look at Ham just a moment in verse 6. *"And the sons of Ham; Cush...."* Who did I say that was? Ethiopia, Somalia, and Sudan. Look at the next one in verse 6, Mizraim—that's modern-day Egypt; Phut (or Put)—that's modern-day Libya.

GENESIS 10:8 and 10

> *And Cush begat Nimrod: he began to be a mighty one in the earth.*
>
> ...
>
> *And the beginning of his kingdom was Babel, and Erech, and Accad, and Calneh, in the land of Shinar.*

That's modern-day Iraq. I have just mentioned Arab nations and Ishmael was not on the scene for at least five hundred years. Between Genesis 10 and Genesis 16 is over five hundred years. Ishmael did not father the Arab world.

Where did Ishmael go to live? Genesis 17:20 talks about, in a pre-incarnate appearance, Jesus Christ told Abraham that Ishmael would be the father of one nation. Not the father of many nations. One nation. In chapter 25, it records what happened. Notice where Ishmael went to live:

GENESIS 25:18

And they dwelt from Havilah unto Shur, that [is] before Egypt, as thou goest toward Assyria: [and] he died in the presence of all his brethren.

That is modern-day Arabia, or Saudi Arabia. That's where he went to live.

Whom did Ishmael father?

GENESIS 25:16

These [are] the sons of Ishmael, and these [are] their names, by their towns, and by their castles; twelve princes according to their nations.

I thought I had a problem when I read that, because I said that he fathered "one nation" and this is talking about "nations."

The interpreter of this passage may have used interpolation, because he used the word "castle." This was four thousand years ago. They went to Arabia to live and there weren't any castles in Arabia in that time. In fact, there are no castles in Arabia today. In this passage, the translators inserted what they thought: if a prince is living in a building or something, it must be a castle; they must have had nations.

If you look at the original Hebrew text, the word translated as "nations" is "ummah," (not "goy" or "goyim," for nations). It means "tribes." And the word translated as "castles" means "tents." And the word for "princes" means "chiefs." Now, if you look at the translation in its proper Hebrew text, you see that Ishmael had twelve sons, and they were chiefs of tribes living in tents. That's exactly what you do in Arabia. You are a chief of a tribe living in a tent.

Do you know the meaning of the word "Arab" in Arabic? It means "Bedouin" or nomad. What are those Arabians? King Abdullah of Saudi Arabia wears that white outfit with that odd-looking headdress. He's a Bedouin. What does a Bedouin do? He wanders around in the desert, watching over his sheep and his goats. He has a tent that he lives in, and it's made out of goat hair. It has a transportable system, so that they can put their poles up, and when the grasses are gone from that part of the desert—and grass does grow in the desert, by the way—they can move to greener pastures; so they pull the poles out and they move their tent. It's not a castle. He went to Arabia to live. You know what the word "Islam" means? It doesn't mean peace. "Salaam," in Arabic, is peace. Islam means submission. These princes would go up and take control of their brothers who were other princes and they would bring them under submission. They were Islamic fighters. You know how they got all charged up to do it? They used hashish in a water pipe. That's hashishim. Assassin. That's where our word comes from, and that culture continued for twenty-five hundred years, to about thirteen hundred years ago.

It was in the sixth or seventh century when Mohammed came to power. He said, "I am a direct descendant of Ishmael. And I'm going to take off all of those gods on the Kaaba," which is the middle of that great coliseum where they march around when they go for their pilgrimage, the Hajj. There were three hundred and sixty gods. He took them all off except one—Allah, which was the moon god. Not the god that I worship in another name. Because their god has no son, it makes that god an antichrist. Islam is a satanic religion that will not co-exist with any other religion. That's why they are doomed (1 John 4:3).

Go back to Ezekiel 38 and let me show you what's going to happen to Islam. What is going to happen is these nations are going to come. Let me tell you when they are going to come. In the last phrase in verse 8, it says they come when the people are gathered out against the mountains of Israel, which have been always waste but they are brought into the land and dwelling safely. In verse 11, it says they will live in unwalled cities. That's when the Antichrist has established a false peace, a pseudo-peace. That's when these enemies attack, when the nation of Israel has laid down their weapons. "Unwalled" cities? That means they laid down their defense. Twenty-five hundred years ago, a wall was in place; today, they have F16 fighters, tanks, and Apache helicopters. When they lay down their weapons, these nations come in to attack. Verse 18 through the rest of chapter 38 talks about how, out of the heavenlies, Jesus Christ will lead an attack on these attacking nations.

EZEKIEL 39:1

Therefore, thou son of man, prophesy against Gog, and say, Thus saith the Lord GOD; Behold, I [am] against thee, O Gog, the chief prince of Meshech and Tubal:

God is against these attacking enemies. Notice what is going to happen in the next verse:

EZEKIEL 39:2

And I will turn thee back, and leave but the sixth part of thee, ...

Now, if you have a different translation, it won't say five out of six are going to be destroyed, but verses 3 and 4 tell the story:

EZEKIEL 39:3-4

And I will smite thy bow out of thy left hand, and will cause thine arrows to fall out of thy right hand.

Thou shalt fall upon the mountains of Israel, thou, and all thy bands, and the people that [is] with thee: I will give thee unto the ravenous birds of every sort, and [to] the beasts of the field to be devoured.

The Tribulation

The rapture of the church is the next main event in God's calendar of activities. There will be a period of time after that, before the seven years start. What did I say started the seven-year period of time? It starts with that peace agreement that is confirmed by Antichrist with Israel. When that happens, Israel lays down their weapons and these nations attack Israel. Then what happens? Five out of every six Islamic people on this earth will be destroyed. When does that peace agreement come? It immediately precedes the seven-year Tribulation.

Why does this have to happen? Where was the Antichrist when he comes back in Daniel 11? He was in the city of Rome. What was he doing? He was putting together a one-world false religion, according to the seventeenth chapter of the book of Revelation. So he establishes the peace, he goes to Rome to establish the false church (the harlot church), the nations attack, and those nations are wiped out by five-sixths. Why? Islam will not collaborate with a false religion. Islam is exclusive. Thus, they must be wiped off the face of the earth for Revelation 17 to take place. On 9/11, Pandora's box was opened, and the Islamic terrorist genie escaped. We are not going to put it back in the box. It was the beginning of the end. The rapture takes place, we depart, these nations attack Israel, and they are wiped out. But until that time, until the rapture, they are the force that must be dealt with. That's the time in which we are living today.

Esau and the Palestinians

A Message of Retribution

Now when we come to Ezekiel 35, we are in a portion of the book of Ezekiel that has been set aside to be the message of restoration. In the first thirty-two chapters of Ezekiel, the prophet is giving a message of retribution. He is a watchman. He hears the word from the Lord and then he warns the people. That is what God called him to do in Ezekiel 3: "Hear my word and warn the people of what is coming." In that message of retribution in those first thirty-two chapters, his tongue had been cleaving to the roof of his mouth during these seven-and-a-half years of ministry, except when God wanted to say something through him, He would open up his tongue and allow him to speak that prophecy.

Then, starting in chapter 33 and going through chapter 48 of the book of Ezekiel, it is a message of restoration. We have looked at the restoration of the Jewish people. In chapter 33, it starts the message of restoration. Eighteen times in chapter 34, God talks about going to find the people, the Jewish people, and bring them back into the land. In chapter 36, He talks thirty-five times about the land. In chapter 37, He talks about them being restored. In chapters 38 and 39, He talks about the destruction of their enemies. In chapters 40 through 46, He uses two hundred and two verses to detail all that is going to be put together in that Temple that He is going to build. In chapters 47 and 48, He talks about the dividing of the land and giving it to the twelve tribes of Israel. So, it is a message of restoration of the Jewish people and their practices.

But, in the midst of this message of restoration, there is a message of retribution once again. Chapter 35 is a message of retribution pronounced against a certain people and it's as up-to-date as possible to help us understand events unfolding in our world today.

EZEKIEL 35:1-4

Moreover the word of the LORD came unto me, saying,

Son of man, set thy face against mount Seir, and prophesy against it,

And say unto it, Thus saith the Lord GOD; Behold, O mount Seir, I [am] against thee, and I will stretch out mine hand against thee, and I will make thee most desolate.

I will lay thy cities waste, and thou shalt be desolate, and thou shalt know that I [am] the LORD.

Now, that's a pretty tough pronouncement of judgment upon Mount Seir. In this chapter, He gives two reasons for the judgment. Here's the first reason:

EZEKIEL 35:5

Because thou hast had a perpetual hatred, and hast shed [the blood of] the children of Israel by the force of the sword in the time of

their calamity, in the time [that their] iniquity
[had] an end:

So, because they killed the children of Israel, they were going to be totally destroyed, as if they never were. Jeremiah 49:18 says they will be as Sodom and Gomorrah.

Here's the other reason that they are going to be judged so harshly:

EZEKIEL 35:10-12

Because thou hast said, These two nations and these two countries shall be mine, and we will possess it; whereas the LORD was there:

Therefore, [as] I live, saith the Lord GOD, I will even do according to thine anger, and according to thine envy which thou hast used out of thy hatred against them; and I will make myself known among them, when I have judged thee.

And thou shalt know that I [am] the LORD, [and that] I have heard all thy blasphemies which thou hast spoken against the mountains of Israel, ...

When they speak against the Jewish people, God considers that blasphemy. And He says that He will judge them for that:

EZEKIEL 35:13-14

Thus with your mouth ye have boasted against me, and have multiplied your words against me: I have heard [them].

Thus saith the Lord GOD; When the whole
earth rejoiceth, I will make thee desolate.

He pronounces a judgment upon Mount Seir.

Identifying Mount Seir

Mount Seir's judgment here, in the middle of a message of restoration, is very strong. I don't believe you can speak any stronger words against a people than are found in Ezekiel 35. But who is Mount Seir? It would probably behoove us, since this is such a profound pronouncement of judgment, to find out who Mount Seir is. So, go to Genesis 25 for information that will help us determine who Mount Seir is. Of course, you have to go back to the book of Genesis, the book of beginning, to start understanding prophecy.

Genesis 25 is a very important prophetic chapter in God's Word. It gives you all of the children of Abraham, and all of their families. We are only going to look at one family, however, and that is the family of the son of promise, Isaac.

GENESIS 25:19-20

And these [are] the generations of Isaac,
Abraham's son: Abraham begat Isaac:

And Isaac was forty years old when he took
Rebekah to wife, ...

Rebekah was from a place called Syria. He chooses her to be his wife. I want you to notice what God does.

You know, I'm sure God laughs. Psalm 2 says He laughs, and so I'm sure He has joy in some of the things He does. I just want you to notice what He did here to old Isaac. Remember Isaac's mother, Sarah? She had a barren womb. So what does God do? God gives Isaac a wife with the same problem.

GENESIS 25:21

> And Isaac intreated the LORD for his wife, because she [was] barren: and the LORD was intreated of him, and Rebekah his wife conceived.

Now what I also think is very funny is this: here is Isaac, who wanted a son so he could continue his family. I don't know if Isaac over-prayed or if the Lord was just having fun, but instead of giving him one son, He gave him two at one time. The first twins in the Bible. Notice in the next verse, his wife has conceived and Rebekah is with child.

GENESIS 25:22

> And the children struggled together within her; and she said, if [it be] so, why [am] I thus? And she went to enquire of the LORD.

The Jacob/Esau Conflict: Then and Now

Now Rebekah had two boys within her womb. They were struggling, and she didn't understand why this was going on, so she went to the Lord and asked, "Why is this happening, Lord?" The Lord responds to her prayer, answering her question, but at the same time, He gives her a prophecy that is very unique and very important for us to understand.

GENESIS 25:23

And the Lord said unto her, Two nations [are] in thy womb, and two manner of people shall be separated from thy bowels; ....

There are going to be two nations; she has two boys in her womb. We know they are Jacob and Esau. These two boys are going to be separated, and they will become two nations in the world. They are going to be two different manner of people.

Notice the last thing He says to her.

GENESIS 25:23 (continued)

... and [the one] people shall be stronger than [the other] people; and the elder shall serve the younger.

That's what God told Rebekah, that the elder would serve the younger.

The Birthright

When you read the rest of this story in the early life of these twin boys, you come to the understanding that Rebekah and her conniving son, Jacob, did everything they possibly could to take away from the firstborn his birthright and his blessing. Actually, none of that had to be done. If she had just simply listened to the Lord, He had already told her, "I am going to give you that." But they had to connive and manipulate to make it happen. She joined with Jacob to do that.

You know what happens, the boys are born and the first one out is Esau. He's not a complete body length first, he's actually held by his heel by Jacob. So there wasn't a complete body length that he was ahead of his brother, Jacob, but Esau was still the firstborn. The firstborn in a Jewish family gets the birthright. That means they will receive all of those privileges as the firstborn and they have the responsibility of carrying the family on to the next generation. Also, when the father is on his deathbed, he will pronounce a blessing upon the oldest son, and God will honor that pronouncement of that particular blessing.

If you continue to read, you know what happened. The boys grew up into their late teens or early twenties. One day, Esau was out in the field, working very tediously at a task and Jacob received a great big beautiful lunch from his mama. He ran out to the field to try and antagonize his brother, Esau. When he got out to the field, his brother was there, sweat pouring down his body. He looked up, saw Jacob, and he said, "Hey, Jacob, give me some of that lunch, I am starving to death." Jacob says, "No way am I giving you any of that lunch. If you want some, you go see mama. Mama made this for me; I'm sitting over here in the shade and I'm going to enjoy this lunch." Finally Esau continued to bicker back and forth with his twin brother, Jacob, and, ultimately,

Jacob manipulated Esau to the point where Esau said, "Okay, okay. You can have my birthright; just give me some of that lunch." He sold his birthright right there. Well, that's the first of the two privileges for the firstborn that Esau gave up. He gave up his birthright.

The Blessing

Now we move along a couple of years to Genesis 27, and we see that the boys have grown older and their daddy has grown older. Isaac is at the point of death and he is almost blind. He can hardly see, and it's time for him to pronounce the blessing upon the firstborn. So he calls Esau in and he says, "Esau, you know how I love venison stew, I want you to go out here and kill me a deer. You kill that deer, you dress it up, make some venison stew, bring it in, and we'll have a great meal together. Then at that point in time, I will pronounce the blessing upon you."

Well, Rebekah heard what Isaac said and ran over to Jacob, "I know how we can get not only the birthright—you've already got that—but we can get the blessing, as well." "How are we going to do that, mama?" "Oh, don't worry about it, I've got it all figured out. Your brother Esau has gone to kill a deer to make some venison stew to take in to your daddy. While he's out there trying to find that deer and make the venison stew, I'm going to dress you up like your twin brother. We'll get one of his old togas; it stinks, and you can put it on and when you walk into your daddy, he is just about blind, he'll just smell and he'll think it's Esau. We'll put some animal skin on your arm, because Esau is very hairy and you hardly have any hair. We'll put it on your arm and if he feels your arm, he'll think you are Esau. And by the way, don't worry about the venison stew, I taught him how to make venison stew. Listen, I've got enough in the freezer. We'll take it out and put it in the microwave; then you'll take the venison stew in, you'll have a great meal with your daddy, and you'll get the blessing pronounced upon you." So they moved ahead to do that, and that's exactly what they did.

Now, Esau walked in with his venison stew immediately after Jacob left, and he heard that Jacob just received the blessing from his daddy. Let's look in on the conversation.

GENESIS 27:38

And Esau said unto his father, Hast thou but one blessing, my father? bless me, [even] me also, O my father. And Esau lifted up his voice, and wept.

Basically, the exegesis of this passage is "he threw a temper tantrum." Esau was very upset about the situation. So Isaac condescended and he said, "Okay, I'm going to give you a blessing."

GENESIS 27:40-41

And by thy sword shalt thou live, and shalt serve thy brother; and it shall come to pass when thou shalt have the dominion, that thou shalt break his yoke from off thy neck.

And Esau hated Jacob because of the blessing wherewith his father blessed him: and Esau said in his heart, The days of mourning for my father are at hand; ....

Esau plotted: "My father will die, we'll mourn for the seven-day period of time, pronounce Sheva upon him"—

GENESIS 27:41 (continued)

... then will I slay my brother Jacob.

The next verse tells us that Rebekah realized this was going to happen. She had a brother who lived up in what we know as modern-day Turkey, a place called Haran, and so she says to Jacob, "You'd better get out of town for a couple of months. Your brother is so upset with what we have done, he's going to try to kill you." So Jacob takes his possessions and goes north to stay with his uncle for a number of years.

Now you know the story. He gets up there, he's getting ready to water his animals one day, and this very good-looking young lady comes walking up. Boy, he falls in love immediately with her, he wants to marry her, and he is manipulated by her like he has been manipulating everybody else. She had a sister not quite as good looking. In fact, she was so ugly, they called her you-gly, and she would take ugly pills every morning when she got up. She was something else. But he ended up marrying her and then he ended up marrying the beautiful one. So, he had a couple of wives, and it's time for him to go back to the Promised Land to be with his family once again. His father-in-law gives him a bunch of spotted cows and they take off, going back to Israel. And that brings us to Genesis 36. All of this is contained within those pages and those verses I did not read. Of course, I read between the lines in some of the description of what went on, but that is the case with any Bible teacher; you have to be able to understand and explain the Word of God and explain it to the people.

Back in Genesis 32, Jacob, on his way into the Promised Land, is over across on the eastern shore of the Jordan River, at the Jabbok River, and there he had a wrestling match all night with Jesus Christ. Before the night is over, He said I want you to be something special to me. Well, at that point in time, Jesus Christ touched the thigh of Jacob, which made him limp for the rest of his life. Why did He touch the thigh? Because that is the strongest muscle in anybody's body. Your thigh muscle is ten times stronger than any muscle in your body. So because of conniving Jacob, Jesus touched the thigh of Jacob and made him lame for the rest of his life. But He also changed his name. He changed it from "Jacob" to "Israel," which means, "I will fight for you." He then was able to work with Jacob from that point on in his life.

Jacob comes back into the land, he crosses over the Jordan River, and he comes to where Esau is living.

When he arrives, there are some things that happen. The Lord is going to have to separate these boys and we are going to see why. But first, in Genesis 36, Esau has his name changed as well. Jacob's name was changed to Israel, Esau's name was changed to Edom.

GENESIS 36:1

Now these [are] the generations of Esau, who [is] Edom.

So, throughout the Word of God, when you read about Edom, you may be reading about Esau. The word "Edom," when used in the Bible, is either talking about Esau himself or it's talking about the area—the geographical area, the southern portion of modern-day Jordan—that Esau is going to be living in. Now notice what happens here as we look at the story unfolding.

The Split

GENESIS 36:6

And Esau took his wives, and his sons, and his daughters, and all the persons of his house, and his cattle, and all his beasts, and all his substance, which he had got in the land of Canaan; and went into the country from the face of his brother Jacob.

He's going to have to leave that area and go someplace else. Now God is going to make a decision at this point in time and, through sovereign selection, He is going to allow Jacob to stay in the Promised Land.

GENESIS 37:1

And Jacob dwelt in the land wherein his father was a stranger, in the land of Canaan.

That is exactly where Jacob is going to be able to stay. Canaan is modern-day Israel. So God gives Jacob Israel at this point in time. I know this is a bit of a history lesson, but just hang in there with me. I'll try to make it exciting. We've got to know the history before we can understand the prophecy.

Now, why did they have to split?

GENESIS 36:7

For their riches were more than that they might dwell together; and the land wherein they were strangers could not bear them because of their cattle.

Both men had become so prosperous, they were not going to be allowed to stay in the same land. The land could not take care of them with their children, with their men servants and their women servants, and with all of their cattle; they were going to have to separate. So Jacob gets Israel, the land of Canaan, and God sends Esau to another location. Notice where he goes:

GENESIS 36:8

Thus dwelt Esau in mount Seir: Esau [is] Edom.

The Red Rock City of Petra

Now let's reflect back on the judgment that was pronounced on Mount Seir, in Ezekiel 35. Mount Seir is defined as the land where Esau went to live. It is the lower third of modern-day Jordan. If you have a map in the back of your Bible, find the location of the Dead Sea (or Salt Sea). Everything between the southern end of the Dead Sea to the Red Sea is Edom on the east side of the Jordan Valley. That is the location that God gave to Esau. You know where his headquarters were? Esau's headquarters were in a city called Petra.

Petra is the most unique city in the world. It was just voted as one of the New Seven Wonders of the World. Because of that designation, it is now a location that all of the world is going to want to visit. I've probably been there more than a hundred times. It is a unique city. It is an impregnable city. It is made of sandstone and the sandstone reflects the colors of the rainbow as the sun moves across the sky. These colors, as you watch them, will change. It's just amazingly beautiful. It's called the Rose-Red City. That's where God sent Esau to live, in Mount Seir. He changed the name of the mountain range to Edom (the mountains of Edom) , and when you read about it in the Bible, that's where he went to live; headquartered in a city called Petra. Now, that's a bit of background.

Esau and the Amalekites

Make note:

GENESIS 36:12

And Timna was concubine to Eliphaz Esau's son; and she bare to Eliphaz Amalek: these [were] the sons of Adah Esau's wife.

The grandson of Esau is Amalek.

In Exodus 12, the children of Israel are led out of the Egyptian bondage. God gave Moses that responsibility, and so he led about two million Jewish people out of Egypt. Soon after their departure, however, Pharoah had a change of heart and ordered the Egyptian military to bring back his slave workforce. When the children of Israel came to the Red Sea, and appeared to have no route of escape, God split the sea and they walked safely across on dry land. Following after them in close pursuit, all of the Egyptian military was destroyed as God closed the sea back up. Then the children of Israel wandered for about a year before they came to the foothills of Mount Sinai.

Israel and the Amalekites

On the way to Mount Sinai, where they would receive the Ten Commandments, they came to a place called Rephidim. That's the location where Moses would hold the rod of God above his head to empower the fighting Israelites (Exodus 17). He had Aaron and Hur standing beside him. In the valley below, the Israelites were fighting the Amalekites, the descendants of Amalek, who is Esau's grandson. So the Amalekites were fighting the Israelites and they were going at it. As long as Moses held the rod of God above his head, the Israelites would win. As he lost his strength and he dropped the rod of God below his head, the Amalekites started to win. As he forced himself to hold the rod of God above his head again, the Israelites would win. Finally, he had Aaron and Hur hold his arms up so the Israelites could win. But not all of the Amalekites were destroyed. Some of those who lived moved into Gibeon, which is near Jerusalem.

In the book of First Samuel is the record of the first king of Israel, King Saul. Samuel is a prophet. He was the one delegated to name King Saul as the first king. Then, in chapter 15, we see that God gives Samuel another prophecy. Let's look at it quickly.

I SAMUEL 15:1-2

Samuel also said unto Saul, The LORD sent me to anoint thee [to be] king over his people, over Israel: now therefore hearken thou unto the voice of the words of the LORD.

Thus saith the LORD of hosts. I remember [that] which Amalek did to Israel, how he laid [wait] for him in the way, when he came up from Egypt.

That was in Exodus 17, the passage we previously looked at. Here's what God told Samuel to tell King Saul to do.

I SAMUEL 15:3

Now go and smite Amalek and utterly destroy all that they have, and spare them not; but slay both man and woman, infant and suckling, ox and sheep, camel and ass.

Kill every one of them. Kill all their animals, kill the babies sucking from their mothers' breasts; kill them all. And Samuel left.

Two days later, Samuel comes back and he walks up to King Saul, "King Saul, you remember what the Lord told me to tell you to do about the Amalekites?" "I do," answered Saul. "Did you kill all the Amalekites?" "I killed them all, the men and the women. I killed all the men and the women, the babies sucking from their mothers, I killed them all. The animals, I killed them all." "What is that noise?" "I don't know." Samuel again asked King Saul, "Did you kill all the Amalekites?" "I did." "Did you kill all of their animals?" "I killed all." "Sounds like the bleating of a sheep to me." "It is. I didn't kill all the sheep, I caught some of them without blemish and without spot; they were perfect. I thought we could offer them in sacrifice." Listen to what Samuel said to King Saul. "King Saul, it's better to be obedient than to offer sacrifice." Boy that will preach. Better to do what God says than to have to confess sin. He said to King Saul, "Did you kill Agag, the king of the Amalekites?" "No, I didn't." "Why didn't you kill Agag?" "Because of his monies, I thought we could use them for our cause." "Where is Agag? Get him over here!" They took him down to Gilgal, just to the east of Jericho. Samuel the prophet walks up to Agag, the king of the Amalekites, "Give me that sword." He took the sword from Agag. He said, "Agag, you see this sword? This sword has made many mothers childless; today it's going to make your mother childless." He took the sword of Agag and he chopped Agag up into little pieces, because when God says to do something, He means it. You don't think I'm making it up, do you? Here's the verse:

I SAMUEL 15:33

And Samuel said, As thy sword hath made women childless, so shall thy mother be childless among women. And Samuel hewed Agag in pieces before the LORD in Gilgal.

It happened out there, in the Judean wilderness.

The Story of Queen Esther—Cast and Script

The book of Esther talks about a king named Ahasuerus. He is the fourth of the Persian kings and richer than all three previous kings put together. Ahasuerus reigned over more than one hundred and twenty-seven provinces. It was a vast piece of real estate, from India in the east to Ethiopia in the west; the known world at the time. He was the Persian king, and his wife, Vashti, was a beautiful and very talented lady. So, he went to Vashti one day and said, "Vashti, I've got all these provincial leaders coming in, I want you to perform for them."

Vashti looked at King Ahasuerus and said, "No way am I going to perform for your provincial leaders!"

King Ahasuerus didn't know what to do. So, he called his counselors together, one of them being Haman, and he asked, "What should we do?"

They said, "King Ahasuerus, you cannot be the king if your wife will not obey you. You are going to have to dethrone her."

So he dethroned her. But then it's time for him to get another wife. So he called for the councilmen to bring in other prospective wives. Well, they are watching and all of a sudden this beautiful girl steps around the corner and he says, "Wow! I want you as my Queen. What's your name?"

"Esther."

She had a cousin named Mordecai. He was a Jew and so was Esther. You see, old King Ahasuerus didn't realize that he was marrying a Jewish girl. Had it not been for such a time as this, when she came into the kingdom, the Jews would have been wiped out.

Esther was crowned queen.

Soon after the royal marriage, Mordecai saved the king's life. He had overheard men planning to kill the king, so he told Queen Esther and she alerted the king.

ESTHER 3:1

After these things did king Ahasuerus promote Haman the son of Hammedatha the Agagite, ...

Soon after his promotion, Haman, now the number two man in the kingdom, came walking through the gates of the city, and there sat this cousin of Esther—Mordecai. Everybody bowed to Haman except old Mordecai. Haman said, "Hey man, you didn't bow to me." Mordecai said, "You are pretty perceptive there, guy. I'm not going to bow to you, either. I don't bow to anybody except God." Now this ticked Haman off, and he devised a plot to kill Mordecai and all of the Jews.

ESTHER 3:6

... Haman sought to destroy all the Jews that [were] throughout the whole kingdom of Ahasuerus, [even] the people of Mordecai.

Long story short, Queen Esther's courage (in revealing Haman's plot to the King) saved the Jews, Mordecai received the overdue gratitude of the king, and Haman was hanged on the very gallows he built for Mordecai.

Okay, you've been going through a history lesson. Look again at this phrase in Esther 3:1: *"Haman the son of Hammedatha the Agagite."* That means Haman was a descendant of Agag, the king of the Amalekites, who was killed in I Samuel 15. The Amalekites were descendants of Amalek, the grandson of Esau. You see the progression? Esau, Amalek, Agag, Haman—all four men wanting to kill Jews, which is the blessing that Esau received from his father, Isaac. By the way, Haman had a great, great, great, great grandson, Herod the Great, who said, "Kill every Jewish boy two years of age and younger; I'll get rid of the King of the Jews. I'm the king of the Jews; the Roman emperor said I was."

The Prophecy of Obadiah

Obadiah is the smallest book in the Old Testament and, in fact, is the smallest book in the entire Bible. That's why it's so difficult to find it. Let me tell you about Obadiah. Obadiah is another pronouncement of judgment upon the Edomites (that's Esau and his descendants).

> OBADIAH 1-2
>
> *The vision of Obadiah. Thus saith the Lord GOD concerning Edom; We have heard a rumour from the LORD, and an ambassador is sent among the heathen, Arise ye, and let us rise up against her in battle.*
>
> *Behold, I have made thee small among the heathen: thou art greatly despised.*

Now, here's the reason He's going to judge these Edomites. Verse 3 says, *"The pride of thine heart hath deceived thee."* Verse 10 states another reason, *"For [thy] violence against thy brother Jacob."* You kill your brother and you are proud because you do it. That's going to bring you down. Go back to verse 3, *"The pride of thine heart."* Here's why they are proud:

OBADIAH 3-4

The pride of thine heart hath deceived thee,
thou that dwellest in the clefts of the rock, whose
habitation [is] high; that saith in his heart, Who
shall bring me down to the ground?

Though thou exalt [thyself] as the eagle, and
though thou set thy nest among the stars, thence
will I bring thee down, saith the LORD."

Petra is a beautiful piece of real estate in Jordan, twenty-five square miles in size. There is only one entrance into Petra—a Siq, which is Arabic for a high, narrow gorge. At some points in this gorge it's only as wide as my arm span, at others it expands out to thirty feet in width, but it meanders for about one-and-a-third miles into the entrance of the city.

The king's highway comes by the entrance of Petra. The king's highway was used by merchants to travel from the continent of Africa over to Mecca, to sell their wares at the Persian Gulf, letting them go out to the rest of the world; or to the Red Sea (both the Persian Gulf and the Red Sea covering the area of Saudi Arabia). So, they would walk by Petra. But the Edomites, who lived in this impregnable city, would lay in wait to rob these traveling merchants. Then the Edomites would run back into the Siq, their protection, as the merchants would follow and try to get them.

Now, if they got into the Siq, what could happen? You see, the walls were five hundred feet high, so the Edomites could be up there with boiling pots of hot water and they could pour it down on their enemies coming in and burn them to death. But if the enemies got through the Siq and made it to the main entrance, you know what it was like in there? The Nabataeans, famous stone carvers from Arabia, had come over to Petra and carved out all types of beautiful edifices inside. There are all kinds of temples and all kinds of home places in there. I mean, the first thing you see when you go in the Siq is this beautiful five-story treasury building carved out of the sandstone. (By the way, the technique for carving sandstone is not from the bottom up, but from the top down, because if you start from the bottom up, it all falls on you. You just die right there.) But, they would lay ropes over the cliffs and they carved this beautiful edifice called the Treasury. If you've seen the Indiana Jones films, that's what he saw when he ran through the Siq on his horse. There is one coliseum inside that will seat about seven thousand people. It's a majestic place. There are man-made and God-made cliffs. So, when their enemies would come, if they were under attack, they could run up in the cliffs and, like eagles in their nest, rest there secure. "Who is going to bring us down? We've got our protection here in our hiding place. Nobody can bring us down." God said, "I can. I can bring you down."

How did He do it? Go to Obadiah 7. Three hundred and fifty years before it would happen, God gave a prophecy to Obadiah to tell him how this would happen.

OBADIAH 7

All the men of thy confederacy have brought thee [even] to the border: the men that were at peace with thee have deceived thee, [and] prevailed against thee; [they that eat] thy bread have laid a wound under thee: [there] is none understanding in him.

What happened? They were having a big banquet. The Edomites had invited the Nabataeans, these stone carvers, to come and sit in the middle of Petra and have a banquet. It was a banquet like you've never seen before in your life. Right in the midst of the banquet, the Nabataeans pick up their swords and they start killing the Edomites. Well, the Edomites must escape and so they run out through the Siq, they turn west, they go across the Jordan Valley, they come into southern Judah. When they get into southern Judah, they become the Idumaeans. They change their names again. Idumaean, which in Greek means southern Judah. A very famous Idumaean was Herod the Great. Everything I've told you to this point is fulfilled prophecy. Verses 1 through 14 in Obadiah—fulfilled prophecy.

OBADIAH 10-11

For [thy] violence against thy brother Jacob shame shall cover thee, and thou shalt be cut off for ever.

In the day that thou stoodest on the other side, in the day that the strangers carried away captive his forces, and foreigners entered into

his gates, and cast lots upon Jerusalem, even
thou [wast] as one of them.

Tisha B'Av, the ninth day of the Jewish month of Av in 586 B.C., is when Nebuchadnezzar came into Jerusalem and destroyed the city of Jerusalem. As Nebuchadnezzar came in, all the enemies of Israel came. Nebuchadnezzar said, "Who would like to burn the Temple down?" Everybody raised their hands. So they cast lots. Folks, three hundred and fifty years before the prophecy happened, Obadiah wrote it down. They cast lots and the lot fell on Esau's descendants, the Edomites. They burned the Temple down. At that point, they sealed their doom forever.

The Future Fulfillment

Everything through verse 14 of Obadiah is fulfilled prophecy. Starting in verse 15, it is prophecy yet to be fulfilled.

OBADIAH 15

For the day of the LORD [is] near upon all
the heathen: as thou hast done, it shall be done
unto thee: thy reward shall return upon thine
own head.

The phrase, "the day of the Lord," is used seventy-two times in the Old Testament. It is talking about a period of time. It has a specific date and a general date. The day of the Lord is any time in history when God personally intercedes on earth in the affairs of man. The general usage of that definition is after the rapture of the church. The rapture is not in the day of the Lord. The day of the Lord starts after the rapture and extends through that seven-year period of time, through the revelation (second coming) of Jesus Christ, and through the thousand-year Millennial Kingdom. But it stops before the Great White Throne Judgment, because that's not on earth. The Great White Throne Judgment, in Revelation 20:11, speaks of a time when Jesus Christ, *"from whose face the earth and the heaven fled away,"* sits on a great throne. So that one-thousand-seven-year period is the day of the Lord in an elongated period of time. But "the day of the Lord" as used in the book of Zechariah, is the day that Jesus steps back on the earth. How do you determine which it is? It's determined by the context, and the context of Obadiah is the day that Jesus Christ steps back on the earth.

OBADIAH 16

For as ye have drunk upon my holy mountain, ...

Is that talking about taking a fifth of Jack Daniels and going up on the Temple Mount and getting drunk? No, it's talking about being intoxicated with power by controlling that Temple Mount. That's exactly what has been done for almost two thousand years. Look at the next verses:

OBADIAH 17-18

But upon mount Zion shall be deliverance, and there shall be holiness; and the house of Jacob shall possess their possessions.

And the house of Jacob shall be a fire, and the house of Joseph a flame, and the house of Esau for stubble, and they shall kindle in them, and devour them; and there shall not be [any] remaining of the house of Esau; for the LORD hath spoken it.

At the return of Jesus Christ, the Jewish people will wipe out the Edomites.

Where are the Edomites Today?

Now, for the rest of the story. I left you with these Edomites running into southern Judah. They became the Idumaeans. Herod the Great was the one responsible for refurbishing that Temple in the time of Jesus Christ. It was called Herod's Temple. In 70 A.D., in accordance with the prophecy that Jesus made, the Roman soldiers came across the Kidron Valley, devastated the Temple, destroyed the city of Jerusalem, and dispersed the Jews into the four corners of the earth. Now, the Edomites (the Idumaeans) joined the Jews, their brothers, to help fight the Romans. The Jews were scattered to the four corners of the earth. Let me tell you where the Edomites were scattered—to a place in the Balkans called Bosnia. That's where these Edomites were sent—to Bosnia. That is 70 A.D.

Let me just quickly jump to the year 1917. General Allenby, commanding officer of the British forces, defeats the Ottomans in the Jezreel Valley. He goes to Jerusalem, and does a mopping up exercise. He then hears from the Ottoman Empire that there is going to be a surrender ceremony. The day is December 11, 1917. I know this story because of Horatio Spafford's daughter. Horatio Spafford wrote the song "It Is Well With My Soul." He was a missionary at the American colony in Jerusalem, and was there that day when this happened. General Allenby got on his white horse and rode over to the Jaffa Gate; he's going to the surrender ceremony. As he approached the gate, he pulled the reins back on his horse and dismounted. His military aide asked, "Sir, aren't you going into the ceremony?" He said, "I am." The aide further inquired, "Why did you get off your horse?" The General responded, "Because one day my Savior, Jesus Christ, will ride a white horse into this city. I am going to walk in." He walked in that day and he took the surrender. But as he did, he looked around, for he knew he had to name somebody as the mayor of Jerusalem.

The Ottoman Empire, who had been in charge of the Middle East for four hundred years, was now out of power. So General Allenby needed to name a new mayor of Jerusalem. He saw a man named Hussein al-Husayni. "Mr. Husayni, you are now mayor of Jerusalem. That's a good-looking young man with you, what's his name?" "Amin al-Husseini, my nephew." Amin al-

Husseini, in 1917, was a young man. When Amin al-Husseini grew up, he was made the Grand Mufti of Jerusalem, the most powerful Islamic leader in all the Middle East. In 1941 he received communiqué from Adolf Hitler. Adolf Hitler said to him, "Come to Berlin. I'll show you how we can rid the world of these Jews." Al-Husseini went to Berlin and Adolf Hitler put him in charge of the Islamic world and their fight to rid the world of Jews. Adolf Hitler had put up a one-million watt power radio station on the Mediterranean coast in Monaco. He told al-Husseini to go on that powerful radio station and call for the Muslims of the world to destroy the Jewish people. He told al-Husseini to go back to Israel and wipe out the Jews. Here's what he said, "Before you go, head over to Bosnia and get the elite commando unit out of Bosnia."

If you know anything about World War II, you know that Adolf Hitler would use a blitzkrieg to take over a country. At the apex of the blitzkrieg would be the elite commando unit from Bosnia. World War I started because of a Bosnian. World War II started because of a Bosnian. They were the elite commando unit that Hitler would use to take over a country. There's a picture in the Holocaust museum of Amin al-Husseini inspecting these elite commandos. He picks them up and he brings them back to Israel. The year is 1948; it's the war of independence.

The United Nations has just told Israel they can become a state among the nations of the world, and the

Arab world says, "We'll wipe them into the sea." The elite commando unit from Bosnia comes in to lead the fight, but they lose. That wasn't the end. Amin al-Husseini had a nephew, too. His nephew's name was Yassar Arafat.

Have you been paying attention? Yassar Arafat, Amin al-Husseini, Hussein al-Husayni, Herod the Great, Haman, Agag, Amalek, Esau. The descendants of Esau are the Palestinian people of today who are still trying to kill the Jew and take their land; exactly what they have done throughout the ages. Obadiah tells us when it's over. Not when they negotiate a peace, but at the time of the revelation (second coming) of Christ. The Palestinians (the Edomites) will be destroyed, and they will be as if they had never been, forever. Never before in history have we been just like this. Never have the Edomites had this power. They will be destroyed, the Palestinian people, when Christ comes back. But before that, seven years of Tribulation, and before that is the rapture of the church.

Temples—Past, Present, and Prophetic

According to verses 13 and 14 in Psalm 132, Jesus Christ has selected Jerusalem as the location where He is going to dwell among His people forever. Chapters 40 through 46 in Ezekiel contain two hundred and two verses with minutely detailed information about the Temple referred to as Messiah's Temple, the Temple that Jesus Christ will build. But we'll come back to Ezekiel and we'll look at that Temple in a moment. First, go to Zechariah, and let me show you why I'm talking about the Temple and why it is important for us to understand the Temple. We will come to an understanding, I believe, of the greatest evidence that the rapture of the church could take place at any moment.

Temples Past

Zechariah is one of those prophets who prophesied after the Babylonian captivity. He had studied twenty-eight years for the priesthood and qualified as a priest while in the Babylonian captivity. He came out of the Babylonian captivity, returned to Israel, and his ministry then was to exhort those people who had returned with Zerubbabel—about fifty thousand of them (49,897, to be exact)—who had come into the land again to build the Temple. Now it will take a period of time. The Babylonian Empire fell in 539 B.C. and they did not finish building the Temple until 515 B.C. It took them twenty-four years to build the Temple, when they should have been able to put it up in two or three years. Solomon built a magnificent Temple and it only took him seven years. They were not talking about building an elaborate Temple like Solomon's Temple, but a simple Temple where they could do their sacrificial activities and their worship service. But they just kept messing around, and got more involved in building their own homes than in building the Temple. Now that has a spiritual application, because many times we get focused on our own projects instead of the projects of the Lord.

Zechariah was one of the two prophets who would prophesy during this time, exhorting the people to build the Temple. The other was Haggai. These men were contemporaries. Haggai was a crusty old guy. Zechariah, on the other hand, was a young, suave guy, who would just kind of encourage Haggai with his nice little smile. There is an approach that can be suave and debonair, one like Zechariah would take. And then there is the approach that Haggai, a crusty old guy would take. That's kind of the guy I model myself after. But Zechariah is one of my favorite prophets. I love Zechariah because I love the conversation that he was able to have with Jesus Christ in chapter 1. In Zechariah 1:12, he meets face to face, person to person with Jesus Christ. Now I say that because it was a pre-incarnate appearance of Jesus Christ. When it says in the Bible, "Then the angel of the Lord," it's talking about a pre-incarnate appearance of Jesus Christ, El-Shaddai.

Notice what He says to Zechariah in this face-to-face meeting that they had.

ZECHARIAH 1:14

So the angel that communed with me said unto me, Cry thou, saying, Thus saith the LORD of hosts; I am jealous for Jerusalem and for Zion with a great jealousy.

In the Hebrew text, the flavor there is, "I am aggressively possessive for the city of Jerusalem." That is a bit stronger than the word jealous. I am aggressively possessive for the city of Jerusalem. Then in the first part of verse 15:

ZECHARIAH 1:15

And I am very sore displeased with the heathen [that are] at ease: ....

The flavor in the Hebrew there would be, "I am very sore displeased with those who are arrogantly secure in controlling the Temple Mount, controlling the location where I'm going to come back."

Temple (Mount) Present

Now, that is the case. That gold-domed building that stands on the spot where the first Temple stood and where the second Temple stood has been there thirteen hundred and twenty-one years. It was built in 691 A.D. The first Temple stood there for four hundred years, the second Temple stood there for six hundred years; a total of one thousand years. But those who control that sacred spot, the most sacred piece of real estate in all of creation, have grown arrogantly secure with their possession.

Temples Prophetic

The Lord tells Zechariah what He is going to do.

ZECHARIAH 1:16

Therefore thus saith the LORD; I am returned to Jerusalem with mercies: my house shall be built in it, saith the LORD of hosts, and a line shall be stretched forth upon Jerusalem.

Now, though he had a ministry twenty-five hundred years ago to the Jewish people who had returned from the Babylonian captivity and was exhorting them to build the Temple, all prophecy has short-term fulfillment and/or a long-term fulfillment. We know He is talking about the future because it says He is going to come to Jerusalem, and He is going to build His Temple in that location.

In the sixth chapter of Zechariah, we have the information that, indeed, this coming prophetic Temple that is going to be built is going to be built by Jesus Christ.

ZECHARIAH 6:12

And speak unto him, saying, Thus speaketh the LORD of hosts, saying, Behold the man whose name [is] The BRANCH; and he shall grow up out of his place, and he shall build the temple of the LORD:

"The Branch" is one of the names for Jesus Christ. Now, the next verse is going to tell us for sure that this is who it is talking about. Jesus Christ is going to build this Temple and I'll point out the time when that is going to take place.

ZECHARIAH 6:13

Even he shall build the Temple of the LORD; and he shall bear the glory, and shall sit and rule upon his throne; and he shall be a priest upon his throne: and the counsel of peace shall be between them both.

So He is going to be ruler of the entire universe, all of creation, dominion given to Him, a kingdom that will last forever, He will be King of kings and He will be Lord of lords. In addition to that, He will be the High Priest. A high priest not after the order of Aaron, but after the order of Melchizedek, He will be the High Priest in that Temple. So Jesus Christ is telling Zechariah, "I will return. I will build My Temple."

Temple Prototype—the Tabernacle

The initial desire to create a place of worship for the Jewish people would take place while they were traveling during the forty years of wandering in the wilderness. In the book of Exodus, chapters 25 through 40, we see God giving Moses all the instructions on how to build the Tabernacle, every aspect of it. Instructions for building the Ark of the Covenant start in Exodus 25:10. Specifications for the table of showbread and the accompanying serveware start in Exodus 25:23. The golden candlestick, which is the menorah, or the seven-branched candelabra, starts in verse 31; how the curtains should raise, in chapter 26; and more. He tells them how to dress themselves as they will be involved in the priesthood, starting in chapter 28; what the high priest should wear, about the holy crown, the 24-karat golden crown that will fit on their heads over the items that they will be wearing, and what the altar should look like. All through here we see a description of the Tabernacle, which would be the prototype for the coming Temples.

The Tabernacle was a transportable worship center that they used during their forty years of wandering in the wilderness. When they came across the Jordan River, about thirty-five hundred years ago, they came in to capture the land. They captured the city of Jericho first, then moved onto Ai and captured that location. They went up to Shiloh and set up the Tabernacle. You can visit these places on one of our tours to Israel. We go up to Shiloh and we go out to the location where, for three hundred and fifty years, they erected a Tabernacle in Israel for the purpose of housing the Ark of the

Covenant. Thus the Ark of the Covenant would have rested there in Shiloh, in the center part of the state, basically, in Samaria during those three hundred and fifty years when they were in the land at first. You remember, of course, what happened there. The Philistines came in and they took the Ark of the Covenant, because Ichabod was written over all that they were doing. ("Ichabod" is a Hebrew word that means "the glory of the Lord is gone.") They had corrupted themselves during that time. The Philistines kept the Ark of the Covenant for seven months. They decided they were going to get rid of it when they had some physical problems. Actually, what they had was hemorrhoids—that's exactly what the Scripture says—and they didn't have anything to deal with them; so they gave the Ark back. Ultimately, after one hundred and twenty years, King David went down to Kiryat Ye'arim, which is on the Jerusalem-Tel Aviv highway, and got the Ark of the Covenant. He brought it into the city of Jerusalem where he erected a Tabernacle to temporarily house the Ark of the Covenant. Then King Solomon, according to the Davidic covenant fulfilling that promise, built the first Temple.

The First Temple—Solomon's Temple

In Second Chronicles, we see the record of King Solomon building the Temple.

II CHRONICLES 3:1

Then Solomon began to build the house of the LORD at Jerusalem in mount Moriah, where [the LORD] appeared unto David his father, in the place that David had prepared in the threshingfloor of Ornan the Jebusite.

In the twenty-first chapter of First Chronicles, it says that King David purchased the threshing floor of Ornan the Jebusite, which was at the peak of Mount Moriah. That is the location where the Holy of Holies is. That's that stone where God created Adam, and it's the location where Abraham brought Isaac and offered him, or attempted to offer him in sacrifice, and it's the location at the peak of Mount Moriah where King Solomon would build that Temple.

Between II Chronicles 3 and II Chronicles 36 is a four-hundred-year period of time. Solomon's Temple would stand until Nebuchadnezzar came in and destroyed it, which is recorded in II Chronicles 36.

The Second Temple—Herod's Temple

In the first chapter of Ezra, God raises up Zerubbabel, through the pleasing presentation of monies and privilege, to go back to Jerusalem and rebuild the Temple. Cyrus, king of the Persian Empire, allows Zerubbabel to select a group of people, about fifty thousand of them, to go into Jerusalem. Remember, I was telling you that Haggai and Zechariah were prophets during this time; notice in the fifth chapter:

EZRA 5:1

Then the prophets, Haggai the prophet, and
Zechariah the son of Iddo, prophesied unto the
Jews that [were] in Judah and Jerusalem in the
name of the God of Israel, [even] unto them.

These prophets were encouraging those who were
building the Temple. In Ezra 6, we see the dedicatory
services when the house is built and that is the second
Temple.

Now that second Temple would stand until 70 A.D.,
when it was destroyed by the Roman army. They came
across the Kidron Valley, went into the Temple complex,
and devastated the Temple. In fact, the prophecy that
Jesus had made, which said there would not be a stone
upon a stone, was uniquely fulfilled by the Roman army.
General Titus and his men had been bivouacked up on
the Mount of Olives for about three months, and morale
was low. So, he challenged them by saying, "You see that
building?" At twenty-one stories high, it was hard to
miss. The rabbis during that time said, "If you've never
seen Herod's building, you've never seen a beautiful
building." Herod's Temple was just simply a beautiful
building. It was covered with pure 24-karat gold, which
molded into the stones; it was majestic on the Jerusalem
skyline. As they started across the Kidron Valley,
General Titus made this announcement. He said,
"Gentlemen, all of the gold on that building is yours, go
get it." They went across that Kidron Valley and they
literally ripped that building apart, stone by stone, to

get the gold off of the stones that covered that beautiful building, thus fulfilling the prophecy of Jesus that there would not be left a stone upon a stone. Now we come to that conclusion by the archeological findings on the Temple Mount and what took place and how that all unfolded, and also by the writings of Josephus, who was the Jewish historian at that time.

So that was the end of the Temple. In 70 A.D., that last Temple, the second Temple of the Jewish people, was destroyed. But God had a plan for destroying that Temple and His plan was that all of the genealogy should be destroyed. The genealogies were kept inside the Temple complex and that destruction would guarantee that nobody could have a written genealogy, which is a record of how the family lifeline should come to the Messiah, the person of Jesus Christ. So, He had the Temple taken out. The other reason for the destruction was that He became the final sacrifice, whereas those Temple sacrifices were for covering sin. Yom Kippur, the day of atonement, the day of covering, would only cover those sins for one year. It did not take them away completely, but that is what Jesus had done with His ultimate sacrifice. And so, they did not have to have that anymore, and that's why He allowed the Temple to be destroyed. We know He's going to build another Temple, because of what He said in Zechariah 1, "I will come back and I will rule and reign from that Temple and I will be the high priest after the order of

Melchizedek, from that particular Temple." That Temple is going to be built and that's what we have.

Now let's go back to Ezekiel 40. That's where we find a description of what is going to be built and set up in the city of Jerusalem, so Jesus Christ can rule and reign. Notice our timeline through the end times. Creation was six thousand years ago. We come along for four thousand years: Jesus Christ comes, dies, is buried, resurrects, goes to Heaven. We come along for two thousand more years: the rapture of the church (the next main event), the seven-year Tribulation period—a terrible time of judgment—leading up to the revelation (second coming) of Jesus Christ, when He returns to the Mount of Olives. What happens when He comes back?

The Four Jewish Spring Feasts

Jesus Christ fulfilled the spring feasts, the first four of the seven Jewish feasts.

He was crucified on Passover; at 3 p.m. Passover evening. Do you recall what they did that evening before? They went and held a Passover Seder. That always is the special meal remembering the Passover that takes place, and that happens in the evening. Since the Jewish day begins in the evening and goes through the next sundown, it was Passover when they had the Passover Seder. And at 3 p.m. in the afternoon on Passover, Jesus Christ was crucified.

He was buried on Unleavened Bread, which basically speaks of separation.

He was resurrected on First Fruits. The Bible says in Leviticus 23 that First Fruits was for the celebration and honoring of God with the first fruits of the barley harvest. Pentecost was the wheat harvest, First Fruits the barley harvest. So they would bring the first of the crops from the barley harvest and take it to the Temple and offer it to the Lord in thanksgiving for providing for them. Well, First Fruits is to be the Sunday after Passover has taken place; the day after the Sabbath, the morrow after the Sabbath. So, First Fruits was the day that Jesus Christ resurrected. Remember what it says in I Corinthians 15, "Jesus is our First Fruits." So He fulfilled that ministry and that Jewish feast.

He sent the Holy Spirit on Pentecost. Fifty days after his resurrection was the Feast of Pentecost. He had promised that the Holy Spirit would come to teach and that would be his ministry, to lift up Jesus Christ, and that was fulfilled, as well.

So with those first four Jewish feasts in the spring, Jesus Christ fulfilled all the prophecies relating to the Jewish feasts, in the proper day sequence.

The Three Jewish Fall Feasts

When Jesus Christ comes back, He is going to fulfill the last three Jewish feasts. There are three Jewish feasts in the fall: the feast of Rosh Hashanah (the Feast of Trumpets); the feast of Yom Kippur (the Day of Atonement); and then the Feast of Sukkot (the Feast of Tabernacles). He will fulfill all of those feasts.

Sometimes, mistakenly, people say that the rapture of the church (since there will be a trumpet blown at the rapture) is the fulfillment of Rosh Hashanah, or the Feast of Trumpets. That is not the case, because these are Jewish feasts. It has nothing to do with Christians. These are Jewish feasts to be observed by Jewish people. The Feast of Trumpets will be fulfilled when Jesus Christ steps back on the earth. In Matthew 24:31, Jesus instructs the angel to blow the trumpet and call a solemn assembly. So when Jesus Christ steps back on earth that will be the fulfillment of the Feast of Trumpets.

During the "Ten Awesome Days"

Yom Kippur is ten days after the Feast of Trumpets. That ten-day period of time is referred to by the Jewish people as the "Ten Awesome Days"; awesome, as in full of solemn wonder. During that time, Jesus—who will have stepped back on the earth—is going to be very busy. What is going to happen, according to Zechariah 14, is that all the nations of the world will gather in Jerusalem. We call it the battle of Armageddon. It is more appropriately called the campaign of Armageddon, because it starts in Jerusalem, not in the Jezreel Valley at Armageddon. All the nations of the world gather at Jerusalem.

I would say maybe one hundred nations with one million soldiers apiece will gather there; that's one hundred million soldiers. Today, there are at least one hundred ninety-two nations in the world, according to the United Nations. But, to be conservative, I'm just counting half of them. They will gather at Jerusalem. Jesus steps down. The Mount of Olives opens up, moving north and south, and that gives Him a valley to go to the Jezreel Valley. It is ninety-seven miles from Jerusalem to Megiddo, where the battle is going to be headquartered in the Jezreel Valley. They are not going to have aircraft carriers and they are likely not going to have helicopters. Remember what is going to happen in the preceding seven-year period of time—a lot of wars. Everything is going to be destroyed, so they will be, as the Bible talks about, on horseback. They are going to move up to the Jezreel Valley to prepare for the final battle. While that is going on, Jesus Christ is going to rebuild the city of Jerusalem. Right now, the size of Jerusalem is approximately eight-and-a-half square miles. Look at Ezekiel 45:1-6, where he is talking about building this location, the city of Jerusalem.

The New City and New Temple

The city of Jerusalem is going to be twenty-five hundred square miles—fifty miles on each side. When you look at the state of Israel, from the Mediterranean coast in Tel Aviv over to the Jordan River is approximately seventy-six miles. So, Jerusalem itself is going to be two-thirds of that. It's going to be fifty miles wide, and fifty miles long; that's twenty-five hundred square miles. And it's going to be lifted up. Zechariah 14 talks about it, Ezekiel 45 talks about it—it's going to be lifted up. Above that is going to be the Temple Mount.

EZEKIEL 42:20

> *He measured it by the four sides: it had a wall round about, five hundred [reeds] long, ...*

A reed is approximately ten feet, so that would be five thousand feet; five thousand two hundred eighty feet is the distance of a mile, so basically this will be a mile square. The Temple Mount is now approximately three football fields in size. The whole old city of Jerusalem, inside the wall, is approximately one mile square. So the Temple Mount is going to be lifted up above the city of Jerusalem, and it will be prominent there on the Jerusalem skyline. The details in Ezekiel 40 through 46, tell us that the Temple is going to stand approximately twenty-one stories high. It's one hundred cubits high, and a royal cubit is what is used here. A regular cubit is from the elbow to the tip of the finger, or eighteen inches. A royal cubit is twenty-one inches, so that would be one hundred seventy-five feet high. That's approximately twenty-one stories high that this Temple is going to be.

There are many interesting things in here about this Temple, but when it will be built is during that ten-day period of time following His return. He comes back on Rosh Hashanah, the Feast of Trumpets. Ten days will pass before Yom Kippur comes. In that time, He is going to build the Temple. He's going to rearrange Jerusalem, rearrange the Temple Mount, build a twenty-one story high Temple, and then He will get ready to go to the battlefield. The campaign of Armageddon will take place, He will go over to Petra, and He will gather in those Jews who found refuge in Petra.

The Bible says the blood will flow as high as the horses' bridles for one hundred seventy-six miles. I take that to be literal. If you have one hundred million soldiers in the battlefield at Jezreel, that will be six hundred million quarts of blood. If you do the numbers on it, that's fifty quarts of blood for every foot for one hundred seventy-six miles. That's about as high as the horses' bridles, so I take that to be literal. By the way, it's one hundred seventy-six miles from Megiddo in the Jezreel Valley to the entrance of Petra, where He is going to keep those people. Isaiah 63 says, "Who is this that cometh from Bozrah? Like He's been treading the winepress of the fierceness of the wrath of almighty God, His white robes are sprinkled with blood." It's Jesus Christ. He said, "I am He that was going, took care of all that needed to be taken care of." He goes and He brings His Jews back. He brings them from the east.

Ezekiel gives information about how He is going to come back.

> EZEKIEL 43:1-2
>
> *Afterward he brought me to the gate, [even] the gate that looketh toward the east:*
>
> *And, behold, the glory of the God of Israel came from the way of the east: ....*

Petra is east of the city of Jerusalem. He's talking about coming by the way of the eastern gate.

EZEKIEL 43:4

And the glory of the LORD came into the house by the way of the gate whose prospect [is] toward the east.

EZEKIEL 43:7

And he said unto me, Son of man, the place of my throne, and the place of the soles of my feet, where I will dwell in the midst of the children of Israel for ever, and my holy name, shall the house of Israel no more defile, [neither] they, nor their kings, by their whoredom, nor by the carcases of their kings in their high places.

He is coming in. He's walking into the Holy of Holies on the day of Yom Kippur

Jesus Christ—Our High Priest

What did the high priest do on a yearly basis? He was the only one allowed to go into the Holy of Holies— taking the blood in, pouring it on the mercy seat on the Ark of the Covenant. Jesus Christ never walked into the Holy of Holies while here on earth. He took His blood into the Holy of Holies in the Temple, the original Temple in the heavenlies (Hebrews 8). So there He went into the original. But the eighth and ninth chapters in Hebrews tell us that everything on earth is simply a replica of that original in the heavenlies. So He went into the Holy of Holies there, but He will come back to earth; and when He brings the Jews from Petra, He will walk into the Holy of Holies and He will then become High Priest, after the order of Melchizedek.

Hebrews 9:24-27 tells us that once, in the end of time, Jesus will do what the priests had to do on a yearly basis. He once will walk into the Holy of Holies. By the way, Zechariah 3:9 says that the Jews are saved in a day. All of those He will bring out of Petra are saved; one-third of all the Jews. Two out of every three Jews, according to Zechariah 13:8, will be killed. One-third will be protected at Petra. And all one-third will come to know Christ as Lord and Savior, according to Zechariah 13:9. On that day when He walks into the Holy of Holies, all of them are saved in one day. By the way, that's what Yom Kippur was. Yom Kippur was the day of atonement for the Jewish people. That was the entire nation; national salvation. Passover was individual salvation.

The Feast of Tabernacles

There will be a four-day period before the next event, and the Feast of Tabernacles. Do you remember when Peter, James, and John went up on the Mount of Transfiguration with Jesus Christ there at Caesarea Philippi? What did Peter say when he saw Moses, Elijah, and Jesus in their glorified bodies? He said, "Let's put up three Tabernacles." Now that's not talking about putting up a statue to honor these men. It's talking about putting up a sukkah. The word in Hebrew for Tabernacle is "sukkah." A sukkah is a thatched hut, which is what they lived in when they were traveling in the wilderness. You put up four poles, you add a framework above, and then you place tree limbs on top. That's how they protected themselves from the sun and the weather while wandering in the wilderness. At the Feast of Tabernacles, they put up a sukkah just outside their homes, so they could live, or eat, or spend the evening, or have fellowship in the sukkah for the seven days. Well, that is representative of the kingdom. That's what Peter thought was happening. He saw them, and Jesus had said, "You shall not die, some of you, before you see me come into my kingdom." Peter said, "Man. We are in the kingdom, let's put up a sukkah. Let's celebrate." That's the Feast of Tabernacles. That is exactly what this is talking about.

So Jesus Christ, as He fulfilled the first four Jewish feasts in the spring, in the proper day sequences, will likewise fulfill the three Jewish fall feasts when He returns. He comes back on Feast of Trumpets, He walks into the Temple on Yom Kippur (the Day of Atonement), and the Tabernacles celebration begins with the Millennial Kingdom. That's when He will rule and reign from that Temple He builds.

Messiah's Temple

Let me show you a couple of differences between Messiah's Temple and the previous ones (the

189

Tabernacle and the first and second Temples). His is a different Temple, and we can know that this Temple has not yet been built because of the description given. Let me just tell you a couple of things. First of all, in this Temple that Jesus Christ talks about, there is no wall of partition around the Temple. In the previous Temples and the Tabernacle, there was a wall of partition, and it was about waist high. The purpose for the wall of partition was to keep the Gentiles from going into the Temple complex. However, there is no wall of partition here. Why not? Jesus Christ said, "When I died, was buried, and resurrected, I took the wall of partition out and made two people one, so they can have access to the Temple." When you step into the holy place and look to the right, there is no table of showbread; that twelve-loaved-high table of showbread will not be there in this Temple, this Messiah's Temple. Jesus Christ said, in John 6:35, "*I am the bread of life*"; and that's what the table of showbread was looking toward. Every piece of furniture in the Temple looked to Jesus Christ. There is no menorah, the seven-branched candelabra. In John, chapters 8, 9, and 11, Jesus Christ said, "*I am the light of the world.*" There's no veil in this Temple. Why? When Jesus Christ was crucified, the veil rent from top to bottom, giving us access to the Holy of Holies. You step into the holy place; there is no Ark of the Covenant. The Ark of the Covenant was a model of Him to come and when you have the real thing, you no longer need the model. Jesus Christ will rule and reign as the Ark of the Covenant, as the mercy seat, in the Holy of Holies.

The Tribulation Temple

I've had the privilege and opportunity to talk with people who are preparing to build the next Temple in Jerusalem. Rabbi Israel Ariel and Rabbi Chaim Richman are from the Temple Institute. I know them both personally. I've been in Chaim Richman's home. He's been on our television program a number of times, and he's on my video, "Ready to Rebuild." I've had great conversations with him, because the Temple they are preparing to build is a replica of Herod's Temple. The great Jewish sage, Maimonides, prepared all the information that they are following to build that Temple. But that's not the Temple that Ezekiel has described. One of their biggest hang-ups is found in Ezekiel 43:13: *"And these [are] the measures of the altar after the cubits: The cubit [is] a cubit...,"* and he talks about the altar. The altar was that two-story high complex outside of the entrance to the Temple where they would offer the animals. It had four horns on it— the four horns of the altar. In the Tabernacle and in the first and second Temples, that altar—fifteen feet high— had a ramp that would lead from the south going up to the north, ascending up to the top of the altar itself. Now there was a reason for that. The reason God had them build this altar with a ramp from the south going to the north is because, during the time of the Tabernacle and the first and second Temples, there was a lot of sun worship; so, this design meant that they would not be looking at the sun. If that ramp had been positioned from the east to the west, when the sun was setting, they would have looked at the sun and been able to worship the sun. If it had been positioned from the west to the east, when the sun was rising, they would have looked at the sun and been able to worship the sun. Thus, they put the sloped ascension to the top of the altar from the south to the north. But I want you to notice something. Look at verse 17:

> EZEKIEL 43:17
>
> *And the settle [shall be] fourteen [cubits] long and fourteen broad in the four squares thereof; and the border about it [shall be] half a cubit; and the bottom thereof [shall be] a cubit about; and his stairs shall look toward the east.*

What is that talking about?

So, the ramp in the other Temples and the Tabernacle would have been going from the south up to the north, but the stairs for the new Temple are going to be looking out to the east. The stairs will be coming from the west up to the altar. The name of the altar here is "Ariel," which in Hebrew means lion-like, or the lion of Judah. Now get the picture: these priests will walk up the stairs, to the top of the altar, at the lion of Judah, look into the Holy of Holies, and who will they see? The Lion of Judah, Jesus Christ. They will worship the Son when they do that. I tried to explain that to these Jewish scholars and they don't want to accept that. I don't quite understand why they do not believe, but I am grateful that God has opened these unique doors to be able to give them information.

There's one more thing I want to show you in Ezekiel 45. There is going to be a reinstitution of the sacrificial system in this Millennial Temple. Their sacrifices are going to be done throughout the year as described in the Scriptures. In chapter 45, we see at least three sacrifices that will take place. The first one in verses 15 and 18, in the first month, in the first day of the month, to cleanse the sanctuary. Also, in verses 21 and 22:

> EZEKIEL 45:21
>
> *In the first [month], ...*

—which would be Nissan—

> EZEKIEL 45:21 (continued)-22
>
> *... in the fourteenth day of the month, ye shall have the passover, a feast of seven days; unleavened bread shall be eaten.*
>
> *And upon that day shall the prince prepare for himself and for all the people of the land a bullock [for] a sin offering.*

The sacrificial system will be reinstituted. But who is going to do the sacrifice? It's not going to be Jesus

Christ. He is not the prince. He is the king. Who is the prince?

Go back to chapter 34 for just a moment. Remember those "I wills" that we talked about?

EZEKIEL 34:24

And I the LORD will be their God, and my servant David a prince among them; I the LORD have spoken [it].

King David is going to be resurrected and be co-regent with Jesus Christ at the Temple. Chapter 37 also confirms that that is going to be the case.

EZEKIEL 37:24

And David my servant [shall be] king over them; and they all shall have one shepherd: they shall also walk in my judgments, ...

Then notice at the end of the next verse:

EZEKIEL 37:25

...and my servant David [shall be] their prince for ever.

The word "prince" is used twenty-four times in the book of Ezekiel and it is talking always about King David. So the sacrificial system will be reimplemented during the Millennial Kingdom. For what purpose? Well, you have a communion service. Do you crucify Jesus afresh and anew? The answer is, "No." Why do you do it? Because Jesus tells us in the eleventh chapter of First

Corinthians, *"This do in remembrance of me."* The sacrifices never took away sin in the past. What were the sacrifices for? Looking toward Jesus. During the Millennial Kingdom, the sacrifices are going to be looking back to Jesus and they are going to be in memorial. That's the only thing I can say. Now, if you don't want to believe that, ask Ezekiel. He has the only answer, as God told him it's going to happen. There is going to be a sacrificial system.

That's the Temple in the Millennial Kingdom. The reason I think it's important that you've been able to read some of this and start to study it, is because we are going to be ruling and reigning with Christ from that Temple. We are going to be hanging around that Temple. You had better know about it. You know there are one hundred sixty-eight verses about the birth of Jesus Christ. In Matthew 1 and 2 and Luke 1 and 2 are four chapters; one hundred sixty-eight verses about the birth of Jesus Christ. I would venture to say that everybody knows all about the birth of Jesus Christ. I wonder how many know about the Temple? The importance of what it's going to be. We are going to be there, we are going to be operating it. We ought to know something about what it's going to be like.

But wait a minute. There's a very interesting verse tucked away in Daniel 9 that talks about the seven-year period of time. (The "he" in this passage is the Antichrist.)

DANIEL 9:27

And he shall confirm the covenant with many for one week: and in the midst of the week he shall cause the sacrifice and the oblation to cease, and for the overspreading of abominations he shall make [it] desolate, ...

This is the Abomination of Desolation. Thus, for Abomination of Desolation and sacrifice to cease, there has to be a Temple in this seven-year period of time. There's going to be a Temple, Messiah's Temple, in the thousand-year kingdom. But there has to be a Temple in the seven-year period of time, because at the midway point, according to Daniel 9:27, that Temple is going to have its sacrificial system cut off and the Abomination of Desolation is going to take place.

Now the original Abomination of Desolation took place in 168 B.C. on December 25th (Keslov 25, the Jewish month of December), when Antiochus IV Epiphanes walked in, slaughtered a pig, threw its innards on the altar, and desecrated the Temple. That was the prototype. That's not going to necessarily happen again. Jesus Christ confirms what I'm telling you in the Olivet Discourse.

MATTHEW 24:15-16

When ye therefore shall see the ABOMINATION OF DESOLATION, spoken of by Daniel the prophet, ...

... flee into the mountains:

So Jesus Christ confirms that, at the midway point, there's going to be an Abomination of Desolation. Second Thessalonians 2:4 tells us that the Abomination of Desolation is going to be when the Antichrist walks into the Temple and sits down in the Holy of Holies and claims to be god. He blasphemes God in the Holy of Holies, the habitation for God Himself. He says, "I am god." That will be the Abomination of Desolation.

Revelation 11:1-2 confirms that there will be a Temple during that time, as well, because in that passage, John is told to take his reed and measure the place for the Temple in the Tribulation period.

What I've just given you is four proof texts: Daniel 9:27, Matthew 24:15-16, II Thessalonians 2:4, and Revelation 11:1-2. There will be a Temple in the Tribulation period.

Preparations for the Next Temple

There is no Temple in Jerusalem today. Where the Temples once stood is where that gold-domed building stands today. That's where the next Temple will stand. But you know, erecting that Temple can be done in six months. That's not the major problem. Of course, you've got to get that Dome of the Rock out of there. That's understood, but that's not the major problem. The major problem was preparing everything that is needed in that Temple. You know what had to be prepared? For starters, they need twenty-eight thousand priests to operate the Temple.

I walked into a yeshiva. It's a place of learning for Jewish young men, like a seminary. Rabbi Nachman Kahana was seated behind his computer, studying the Torah. I asked, "Rabbi, do you use that computer for anything else?"

He said, "I do."

I said, "What?"

He said, "I use this computer for a database of Jews qualified to be priests."

I said, "Wow. Well, why do you have that list?"

"Because we've called them all to Jerusalem."

"To do what?"

"To build a Temple, and they have to be prepared as to how to operate it."

"WOW! Now, wait a minute. Don't these priests have to have special garments?"

He said, "Yes they do. See the garments for the priests have to be made out of one piece of cloth. And they prepared twenty-eight thousand garments for these priests—they are in storage. In fact, my garment hangs in my closet, awaiting my time as priest."

I said, "Wow! Glory to God! Hold it just a moment. What about the implements? You have to have the mizrak."

The mizrak is a pitcher-shaped item that's made out of pure gold or pure silver. It doesn't have a base, it has a point, because if it had a base, you could set it down and the blood would coagulate. This is blood from the sacrifices. It has a point so they can't set it down or it will fall over. The priests have to keep moving it so the blood doesn't coagulate. You need four thousand of them made out of pure gold or pure silver, and they have four thousand of them.

They have the table of showbread, they have the altar of incense, and—just about two years ago—they took one hundred pounds of pure gold and made the menorah, or the seven-branched candelabra.

The Rabbi continued, "It's on display in the Cardo in the old city, in the Jewish quarter of Jerusalem. I could take you there right now, so you could touch it with your hand. It's there." (The menorah has since been moved to a spot overlooking the Western Wall Plaza.)

The Harps of King David

I said, "Wait a minute, Rabbi. I got you, man. What about those harps that King David called for?"

He said, "Go over to number 10 King David Street."

Isn't that a neat address? So I walked over to number 10 King David Street and I walked in and there was Micha and Shushanna Harrari. They had moved from Vermont to Israel. Micha was a finish carpenter. He could make anything with a hammer and saw.

One day, Shushanna, his wife, said, "Micha, my birthday is coming and I would like for you to make me a harp."

Micha said, "Now darling, I would love to please you, but I don't know how to make a harp. I made a guitar, but I don't know how to make a harp."

Now, you know how girls lay it on, "Boohoo! Micha, it's my birthday!"

He said, "OK, quit harping, I'll make you a harp."

He went to the Jezreel Valley, and he walked into a cave. There was a ten-string harp, like King David used to play, carved on the wall. He made a copy of it, and brought it back to Jerusalem. From that copy, he made a ten-string harp. The Jerusalem Post did a story on that ten-string harp. Based upon the research she had done, the reporter wrote that this is the first harp made in two thousand years in Jerusalem.

The next day, an old rabbi showed up; he was in his eighties. He walked in and asked, "Do you have a ten-string harp?"

"I do."

"May I see it?"

"You may."

He held the ten-string harp in his arms and he started to cry.

Shushanna asked, "Rabbi, why are you crying?"

He said, "Because the Talmud says when a ten-string harp shows up in Jerusalem, it's the time for the coming of the Messiah."

And it was there. They now have four thousand harps. That's exactly what King David called for.

The Sanhedrin

In 2005, on the shores of the Sea of Galilee at Tiberius, after fourteen hundred years, seventy Jewish wise men came together. They were experts in jurisprudence, Biblical scholars, and they re-formed the Sanhedrin, which is the group that operates the Temple and elects the high priest. A short time ago, on my radio broadcast, I was talking with Professor Hillel Weiss. He's the spokesperson for the Sanhedrin. I said, "Professor Weiss, what is your latest information?" He said, "Jimmy, we have elected the high priest." Judy and I, when in Jerusalem, had contact with the man who has been elected high priest. I interviewed Jacov Kleinman. He's the head of the center of the Kohanim. They held a conference in Jerusalem of all the men who are priests from all over the world, and they received their final training for this Temple over here.

By the way, in case you think I've been pulling your leg, I've documented everything on my video. Two rabbis on the video said they actually went to the Ark of the Covenant. They came within twenty-five feet of it. I asked, "Rabbis, why didn't you bring it out?" One answered, "We will when we have a place to put it." All preparations have been made for this Temple to go up. There is only one thing that must happen before the Temple goes up: the rapture of the church! And we are out of here! And then they build the Temple. We are that close. The Temple could be built in six months. Everything is ready. Never in the history of the world has everything been ready for the Temple. The rapture takes place—the rapture could happen today!—and they build the Temple, which is what the text says. That's how close.

Final Thought

Are you ready?

From our study of the book of Ezekiel, we see how God is working through the Jewish people today. We see God's retribution for disobedience by the Jewish people, but at the same time we see God's restoration of His people. The Jewish people are returning to the land of their forefathers and the Lord is about to restore the practices of the Jews; it's happening right before our very eyes. Events taking place in the Middle East right now are setting the stage for God's final act to begin.

As I travel across the country and around the world, many people ask me to predict when I think the rapture will take place. My answer is always the same. I predict the rapture will happen...TONIGHT!! There is not one more prophecy that has to be fulfilled; all is ready. I think I'm in pretty good company when I make that prediction. Two thousand years ago, the apostle Paul said that we *"shall be caught up together ... in the air"* (I Thessalonians 4:17). If Paul believed in his day that the rapture was imminent, how can we—who have been witness to the incredible stage-setting for the fulfillment of prophecy that I detailed in this book— doubt that the rapture will soon be at hand? I believe with all of my heart that the rapture is going to happen tonight. But, should you see me tomorrow, or some future tomorrow, and come running up to me and ask,

"OK, Jimmy, <u>now</u> when's the rapture going to happen?" Without missing a beat, I will say again, "Tonight!"

My point is that we need to live like every day is the day of the rapture. And, indeed, nothing is stopping it from happening tonight, or even today.

If you are not a Christian, how can you prepare for the Lord's return? Getting prepared is as simple as A, B, C.

"A" Admit that you are a sinner in need of a Savior to take away your sin. (Romans 3:23)

"B" Believe that Jesus Christ died for you to take away that sin. Believe that He rose from the dead to prove He is who He said He is and can do what He said He would do. Believe that He will save you as He said He would. (Romans 10:9)

"C" Call upon Him to save you. The Bible says, "*FOR WHOSOEVER SHALL CALL UPON THE NAME OF THE LORD SHALL BE SAVED.*" (Romans 10:13)

I believe Jesus Christ is coming very soon. The rapture of the church could take place at any moment! That truth should cause all of us to want to live pure and be productive in light of what is most certainly a soon return of Jesus Christ. Having said that, there is nothing left for me to say after this study except, "Let's keep looking up... Until."

Appendices

Scriptures Index

People Index

Places Index

Subjects Index

About Jimmy DeYoung

Jimmy DeYoung is a prophecy teacher and journalist who travels the country and the world educating the Body of Christ about the future events foretold in God's prophetic Word.

His goal is to equip Christians with the knowledge and understanding of what God's Word says will happen someday soon, so that they can make better decisions today.

Jimmy DeYoung has several ministries to this end: Prophecy Today Radio, the School of Prophets, the Until Newsletter, Shofar Communications, Joshua Travel, and more. Here are a few of his websites:

www.jimmydeyoung.com
www.prophecytoday.com
www.schoolofprophets.org
www.prophecybookstore.com
www.joshuatravel.com

Jimmy DeYoung and his wife of over fifty years, Judy, resided in Jerusalem for twelve years, where he held full credentials as a journalist in the second most populated journalistic city in the world. Arriving there just three days prior to the Gulf Crisis in 1991, he weathered 39 Scud attacks. Jimmy gave reports nationwide on several networks during the Gulf Crisis. Today he continues to have his finger on the pulse of what is considered the media "hot spot" of our time—the Middle East. On his travels throughout the U.S. and around the world, Jimmy brings with him the latest news from out of the Middle East with a unique blend of political, Biblical, and prophetic insight that cannot be found in the media today.

After graduating from Tennessee Temple University in Chattanooga, Tennessee, Jimmy joined with Jack Wyrtzen and Harry Bollback at Word of Life Fellowship in Schroon Lake, New York. There he spent the next twelve years in many staff positions, including staff evangelist, host of Word of Life Inn, and producer of radio programs heard worldwide.

For the next five years, Jimmy was the Vice-President and General Manager of New York City's first Christian radio station, WNYM. During his time at the station, Jimmy was the producer and host of a daily talk program in the #1 media market in America.

Upon first arriving in Israel, moved by the plight of the Israeli people and by the spirit of God, Dr. DeYoung founded the Assembly at Jerusalem, a Bible-preaching church that meets in the Holy City. Today, Jimmy travels the world proclaiming the good news of Christ's gift of eternal life and soon-coming return for His Church, using the means of media, radio, television, books, and the internet, as well as by preaching in churches and assemblies across the globe.

Jimmy has met and interviewed many international leaders, including: Israeli Prime Minister Benjamin

Netanyahu, former Israeli Prime Minister Ariel Sharon, former Israeli Foreign Minister Shimon Peres (now President of Israel), former Israeli Prime Minister Ehud Olmert, former Israeli Defense Minister Moshe Arens, former Jordanian Foreign Minister Marwan al-Muasher, and the late Palestinian leader Yasser Arafat.

Jimmy is seen on the *Day of Discovery* television program, which is produced in the Middle East, and is a frequent guest on *The John Ankerberg Show*. He is also heard daily and weekly on radio and internet, delivering the latest reports from the Middle East on several networks, consisting of over 1,500 stations.

Jimmy is a noted conference speaker in the United States, Europe, and South America, and he devotes several months out of each year to this conference schedule. He has authored the best-selling books *Sound the Trumpets* and *Revelation: A Chronology*, co-authored *Israel Under Fire* with Dr. John Ankerberg, and produced a number of audio and video materials, including his top-selling *Ready to Rebuild*, a documentary on the building of the Third Temple. Jimmy continues to monitor the most current events as they unfold in the Middle East and compares these current events to the prophetic truth of God's Word.

Jimmy had the privilege of receiving his Doctorate from Tennessee Temple University in May of 1996. He also received a Ph.D. from Louisiana Baptist University in May of 2000.

The School of Prophets

Jimmy has a deep desire to have as many people as possible in the Body of Christ understand Bible prophecy, which makes up one-third of God's Word. To that end, he started the **School of Prophets** in partnership with Louisiana Baptist University, which offers both a Masters degree (M.A.) and a Doctoral Degree (Ph.D.) in Advanced Prophetics.

The courses provided at the School of Prophets are derived from Jimmy DeYoung's study of the Bible and he is integrally involved in the school. Jimmy grades papers, evaluates projects, and provides specific feedback to each individual throughout the entire program.

If you are interested in this exhaustive and systematic graduate-level study of Bible prophecy, please visit www.schoolofprophets.org.